Choderlos de Laclos

Les Liaisons dangereuses

† Philip Thody

Emeritus Professor of French,
University of Leeds

UNIVERSITY of GLASGOW
FRENCH AND GERMAN PUBLICATIONS
2003

University of Glasgow French and German Publications

Series Editors: Mark G. Ward (German)
Geoff Woollen (French)

Modern Languages Building, University of Glasgow,
Glasgow G12 8QL, Scotland

Originally published by Edward Arnold Ltd., 1970.
Second edition first published 1975.
Revised and augmented reprint published 1991; reprinted 1998, 2003.

Printed by Universities' Design and Print, Glasgow.

ISBN 0 85261 317 2

Contents

Note on editions

Laurent Versini's edition of the *Œuvres complètes* (NRF Gallimard, 'Bibliothèque de la Pléiade', 1979) can be considered definitive. Citations from this, carefully differentiated from comments and judgments passed in his 1968 book, will be indicated as having been taken from the **reference edition.** Other contemporary judgments, such as those of La Harpe and Tilly, are more conveniently to be found in the superseded Pléiade *Œuvres complètes,* annotated by Maurice Allem. It was printed several times, and the pagination varies; references made are to the 1959 reprint, which will for brevity be called the **Allem edition.**

The epistolary form ensures that citations can be quickly located in any paperback edition, the major difference being that Roman and not Arabic numerals may head the hundred and seventy-five letters; it is the latter (bracketed, in **bold type**) that appear in this guide. The recently-published Presses Pocket edition, in the 'Lire et Voir les Classiques' collection (1989), has a particularly attractive sixteen-page selection of iconographical material running from the original book cover to stills from the recent Stephen Frears film. The screenplay of this, by Christopher Hampton, has appeared in paperback as *'Dangerous Liaisons': The Film* (Faber and Faber, 1989).

Unless it is stated otherwise, French and English works are published in Paris and London, respectively.

Chapter One

The Critical Problem

Events and interpretations

Les Liaisons dangereuses, a novel in letter form, was
published in late March 1782, ostensibly in Amsterdam but in
fact in Paris. It was immediately successful, and twelve
separate re-editions appeared within the same year. The Queen
herself, it was rumoured, had her own personal copy bound in
plain leather, and there was undoubtedly a strong element of
scandal in the initial success which the novel enjoyed. Perhaps
because of the apparent ease with which real names could be
put on the fictitious characters, the police attempted to ban the
sale of the book, and its author, Pierre-Ambroise-François
Choderlos de Laclos, a middle-aged artillery officer, was
ordered to leave Paris and rejoin his regiment in Brittany. For
over a century he remained virtually identified with his
wicked and cynical hero Valmont, and it was only with the
publication in 1903 of his essays on women's education, and
with the appearance in 1905 of Émile Dard's still definitive
biography that readers of *Les Liaisons dangereuses* could find
out what Laclos himself thought and felt.

He was, before leaving the army in 1788, a capable, hard-
working but not particularly successful officer. Twenty-eight
years after entering the artillery school at La Fère in 1760, he
had still only attained the rank of *capitaine-commandant*
— roughly the equivalent of a major—and he was probably
contrasting his own slow promotion with the rapid
advancement of his aristocratic rivals when he wrote, in his
Profession de foi (1791) on the debate between monarchy and
republicanism:

> On entrera au service à dix-huit ans; on deviendra capitaine
> environ à trente ans; et c'est ici que commence la séparation.
> Celui qui fera son chemin par le choix du roi sera
> lieutenant-colonel à trente-deux ans; colonel à trente-quatre,
> maréchal-de-camp à trente-six et lieutenant-général à trente-huit
> ans.[1]

The implication is that Laclos himself enjoyed no such official favouritism, and Émile Dard's thesis that he wrote *Les Liaisons dangereuses* partly to compensate for his frustrated military ambitions is borne out by the fact that once Laclos had become involved in politics, he seems to have given up literature almost completely. In 1788, he became a kind of public relations officer for the King's cousin, Philippe d'Orléans, and helped him in his intrigues to supplant Louis XVI during the early years of the Revolution. He joined the Jacobin club in 1790, edited their newspaper, the *Journal des Amis de la Constitution*, was imprisoned in 1793 because of his former association with the duc d'Orléans, escaped the guillotine as a result of the fall of Robespierre in July 1794, but still remained in prison until December of the same year.

The eighty or so letters that Laclos wrote to his wife while he was in prison, like the hundred which he sent her while he was away on active service with the army in the early eighteen hundreds, seem at first sight an almost perfect demonstration of T.S. Eliot's contention that:

> Impressions and experiences which are important for the man may take no part in his poetry, and those which become important in his poetry may play quite a negligible part in the man, the personality.

They show a man devoted to his wife, anxious to reassure her, in spite of all the evidence to the contrary, that he is in no real danger, stoical in his own attitude to misfortune, and totally without irony, guile or affectation. Nothing could be more different from the letters in the novel to which he owes his enduring fame, but to which he almost never refers. His concern is solely with his wife, his children, and with the details of the not outstandingly successful military career which came to an end in Taranto, in 1803, after he had served as a general with Napoleon's armies on the Rhine and in Italy, and been given command of the artillery in the French army occupying Naples.

For earlier critics, there was nevertheless a link between Laclos's public life and the atmosphere of his novel. The main plot of *Les Liaisons dangereuses* describes the seduction by the vicomte de Valmont of the virtuous and beautiful présidente de Tourvel, and he is initially inspired by no sentiment higher than a rather perverse delight in making other people behave as he wishes but against their will. His partner and rival, the marquise de Merteuil, is similarly concerned with her own power and prestige, and urges Valmont to seduce the innocent but easily corruptible Cécile Volanges solely in order to satisfy her own desire for vengeance over a former lover, Gercourt, who had abandoned her some time before the action of the novel begins. Both Valmont and madame de Merteuil are totally ruthless in their pursuit of power, and however unjust it may have been for Sainte-Beuve to write that Laclos, 'du moment qu'il fut devenu l'âme du parti d'Orléans, n'eut qu'à appliquer son art et sa faculté d'intrigue à la politique pour en tirer, dans un autre ordre, des combinaisons non moins perverses et vénéneuses',[2] there is at least a surface resemblance between the Valmont who tried all forms of hypocrisy to seduce the présidente de Tourvel, and the Laclos who seems to have felt little compunction in transferring his allegiance from the duc d'Orléans to the Jacobins and from the Jacobins to Bonaparte. Moreover, when Valmont describes his final seduction of the Présidente in exclusively military terms, he seems to have become the ideal wish-fulfilment of the ambitious soldier who spent his twenty-eight years in the army before hearing a shot fired in anger. 'Jugez-moi donc comme Turenne ou Frédéric', he writes to the marquise de Merteuil:

> J'ai forcé à combattre l'ennemi qui ne voulait que temporiser; je me suis donné, par de savantes manœuvres, le choix du terrain et celui des dispositions; j'ai su inspirer la sécurité à l'ennemi, pour le joindre plus facilement dans sa retraite; j'ai su y faire succéder la terreur, avant d'en venir au combat; je n'ai rien mis au hasard, que par la considération d'un grand avantage en cas de succès, et la certitude des ressources en cas de défaite; enfin, je n'ai engagé l'action qu'avec une retraite assurée, par où je puisse couvrir et conserver tout ce que j'avais conquis précédemment. (125)

At first sight, *Les Liaisons dangereuses* seems a perfect example of how real ambitions can be sublimated through imaginative literature, giving life and intensity to a work of art by the very fact that they have been bottled up for so long.

During the nineteenth century, *Les Liaisons dangereuses* was widely regarded as an immoral book written by a wicked man. Little was known of Laclos's private life, and it was common enough practice in Restoration France to regard anyone who had been involved in the revolution of 1789 as thoroughly immoral for that very reason. The remarks made by Sainte-Beuve are an indication of how widespread this attitude was, and in 1834 Charles Nodier actually apologised for quoting Laclos on the grounds that his work reflected a 'less literary but more depraved' period than the late Roman Empire described by Petronius.[3] Even Michelet, sympathetic though he was to many aspects of the Revolution, described Laclos as the personification of vice, and stated that *Les Liaisons dangereuses* was a useful prelude to his career as a 'political scoundrel'.[4] For much of the nineteenth century *Les liaisons dangereuses* was included on the list of books to be confiscated by the police on the grounds that they were immoral, while in early twentieth-century England, George Saintsbury reflected a widely held view when he wrote, in 1917, that Valmont and madame de Merteuil were 'merely disgusting', dismissed their wickedness as 'prosaic and suburban', and refused to discuss *Les Liaisons dangereuses* in his influential *History of the French Novel*. [5] Even as late as 1950, another well-known English critic, Martin Turnell, seemed almost to apologise for including what he described as 'that very great, very unedifying and in England very neglected masterpiece' in his book *The Novel in France*. [6]

There are, however, a number of obstacles to this view of *Les Liaisons dangereuses* as an immoral book, and it has long been quite impossible to accept the opinion that Valmont, whose name so curiously resembles that of his creator, was a self-portrait of Laclos himself. Four years after the publication of *Les Liaisons dangereuses*, on 3 May 1786, at the age of forty-five, Laclos married a young woman of twenty-five, Marie-Soulange Duperré, the eldest of twenty-two children. She had already, on 1 May 1784, borne him a son, Étienne-Fargeau, but there was no question of Laclos behaving as Valmont might have done in comparable circumstances. Marie-Soulange bore him two more children, Catherine-Soulange, in October 1788, and Charles, on 4 June 1795, the latter having been conceived in the prison of Picpus on one of the visits which Marie-Soulange was allowed to make in the freer atmosphere which followed the fall of Robespierre.

He was, from all accounts, a perfect husband and devoted father: René Pomeau begins his article on their conjugal happiness with the entry that appeared in the *Biographie Michaud:* 'Bon fils, bon père, excellent époux',[7] and indeed he wrote to his wife in 1801 that he was thinking of writing a novel on the theme: 'Il n'existe de bonheur que dans la famille.'[8] His essays on women's education, written in 1783 but not published until long after his death, show that he agreed with Rousseau in seeing nature as vastly superior to civilisation, and was a firm believer in equal rights for women. Far from admiring the elegance and sophistication which seem to make madame de Merteuil so attractive, Laclos considered that women should live as spontaneously as possible, and recommended young girls to rely on nothing but early nights, fresh air and a pleasant disposition to improve their natural charms. However much support the ruthless ambition revealed by Laclos's public career might lend to those critics who share his contemporary Tilly's view that *Les Liaisons dangereuses* is 'l'ouvrage d'une tête de premier ordre, d'un cœur pourri et du génie du mal',[9] his private life and expressed opinions on what should be the relationship between the sexes suggest that the novel is not the manual of sexual licence that it first appears. Indeed, the more one looks at *Les Liaisons dangereuses* in the light of Laclos's ideas on women's education and on marriage, the easier it becomes to accept Baudelaire's suggestion that it is a 'livre de moraliste aussi haut que les plus élevés, aussi profond que les plus profonds',[10] and disagree with La Harpe's contention that in the apparently moral ending of the novel: 'Le vice ne trouve donc pas ici sa punition en lui-même, et ce dénouement sans moralité ne vaut pas mieux que le reste.'[11]

The strongest support for a 'moral' reading of *Les Liaisons dangereuses* is nevertheless to be found in the text itself, and especially in the way the atmosphere changes as the plot develops. Initially, all seems gaiety and charm, and the reader easily forgets, in his admiration for the wit and intelligence of the two main characters, how cruel their behaviour really is. The marquise de Merteuil wishes to avenge herself on one of her former lovers, the comte de Gercourt, for having abandoned her. The instrument she chooses is the vicomte de Valmont, who has also been her lover in the past, and her immediate victim is Cécile Volanges, Gercourt's fiancée. Her plan is that Valmont shall seduce Cécile before her marriage, and thus make Gercourt the laughing stock of Paris. Everyone will be told what has happened, and Valmont will also give Cécile such a taste for pleasure that she will proceed to cuckold her husband on every possible occasion.

At first Valmont refuses, arguing that he has more difficult and rewarding things to do. He is trying to seduce the présidente de Tourvel, whose beauty and virtue make her a more 'worthy enemy'(4) than Cécile. It is only when he discovers that Cécile's mother has been warning the Présidente against him (44) that he agrees to madame de Merteuil's plans. In spite of the fact that Cécile has by now fallen in love with a young man called Danceny, he has little real difficulty in seducing her. In what is perhaps the first reference in the European novel to the practice of contraception, he is careful to point out to madame de Merteuil that he has taken no precautions (110), and soon triumphantly announces to her that Cécile is pregnant (115).[12] After a long siege, the Présidente eventually capitulates, and Valmont becomes her lover. Yet while everything seems to be working out even better than both he and madame de Merteuil had intended, more powerful forces within the two main characters are working to bring about their downfall.

It becomes apparent, early in the exchange of letters between madame de Merteuil and Valmont, that each is intensely jealous of the other's exploits. The moment Valmont announces his intentions of seducing the Présidente, the Marquise counters with a long description, clearly intended to make him jealous, of the delights she has been according her present lover, Belleroche (10). His remarks in letter 15 show that she is succeeding, and at the earliest opportunity he counters with his description of the night he has spent with one of his former mistresses, Émilie (47). It is equally obvious from letter 71 that he is trying to make her jealous by the account of his adventure with the vicomtesse de M***, and the whole of the Prévan episode, which dominates Part II of the novel, is an illustration of the rivalry which characterises their relationship. Thus it is Valmont who introduces the episode by what is just as much a challenge as a warning (70), and his next two letters (76; 79) seem intended to spur the Marquise on to further efforts by implying that she is not quite skilful enough to deal with this new situation. His assumption of masculine pre-eminence provokes a long letter in which madame de Merteuil gives a convincing account of her own superiority (81), and she proceeds to prove her worth by taking Prévan as her lover and then making him appear both a fool and a scoundrel (85). Throughout the novel, Valmont tries to assert his power by persuading the Marquise to become his mistress again, while she retains her superiority by insisting that he first of all shows her the Présidente's love letters. Her early realisation that Valmont has in fact fallen in love with madame de Tourvel gives her a much better understanding of his motives than he has himself, and she plays on his vanity until he finally sends the Présidente an extremely cruel letter breaking off their affair. Whether or not the Marquise loves Valmont herself is not entirely clear, and there is at least the suggestion that she is incapable of such an emotion. It is nevertheless obvious that she cannot bear the idea of his belonging to somebody else, and for all her intellectual superiority, it is she who makes the fatal mistake which ruins all her plans.

No sooner has Valmont seduced mademoiselle Volanges than the marquise de Merteuil turns her own attention to Danceny, the young man still romantically in love with Cécile. She is clearly using Danceny to show that she too can seduce people younger than herself, and when Valmont returns to Paris to claim his reward for finally breaking with madame de Tourvel, he finds them together. Rightly suspecting what has happened, he avenges himself by persuading Danceny to break an engagement with madame de Merteuil in order to go and meet Cécile. His vengeance is well within the conventions of the sex war which they have now officially declared, but madame de Merteuil acts less rationally. Furious at being deliberately humiliated by one man and unconsciously insulted by another, she tells Danceny about Valmont's seduction of Cécile. Danceny challenges Valmont to a duel, and kills him. Before he dies, however, Valmont makes one final gesture of masculine solidarity: he hands over to Danceny the whole of his correspondence with madame de Merteuil. The publication of her letters leads to a scene where she is openly humiliated at the Comédie Italienne (173), as well as to the loss of an important lawsuit in which she loses all her money. And, driving the nail rather unnecessarily home, Laclos punishes her still further by a violent attack of smallpox which, as an unnamed marquis remarks, now shows her soul upon her face (175).

This excessively moral ending might, as some critics have suggested, be seen as essentially ironic, if it were not for a number of other features in the actual plot of *Les Liaisons dangereuses* which reinforce the view that Laclos is trying to criticise the behaviour of Valmont and the marquise de Merteuil rather than present them as models. For all her planning, the original object of madame de Merteuil's vengeance escapes unscathed: Gercourt never marries Cécile, and is thus never cuckolded by her. Although saved by a timely miscarriage from having an illegitimate child (140), Cécile is so overcome with horror at the deceit practised upon her by Valmont and madame de Merteuil that she seeks refuge in a convent. There is little doubt in the reader's mind that Gercourt will soon replace her with another blonde heiress, and it is equally obvious that madame de Merteuil missed her revenge only because she gave way to her fury and denounced Valmont to Danceny. With a little more self-control, she could have held off until Cécile was safely married, and it is the height of irony that a woman who claims (81) to have achieved complete mastery over her feelings should ruin her whole life by this one act of signal folly. Valmont has already warned her that 'chacun de nous ayant en main tout ce qu'il faut pour perdre l'autre, nous avons un égal intérêt à nous ménager mutuellement'(153), and hinted that they cannot afford open warfare. Like two rattlesnakes, or two nuclear powers, she and Valmont can survive only if they keep their aggression within certain limits. Yet although it is she who breaks these rules and thus brings about the final catastrophe, she is not the only person in the novel who falls victim to the nemesis which overtakes those who consider that the head can always dominate the heart.

The most striking example of this is Valmont, who begins his campaign against the présidente de Tourvel in order to satisfy his vanity and fill an empty summer, but who soon finds himself much more deeply involved than he intended. His night with Émilie (47), like his adventure with the vicomtesse de M*** (71), can be interpreted as part of a deliberate attempt to reassure himself that he is still the heartless seducer which he prides himself on being, and he seems to admit this when he tells madame de Merteuil that he is going to use Cécile to 'affaiblir, en la partageant, l'impression peut-être trop vive que j'ai éprouvée'(133). He explains his second encounter with Émilie by the same considerations (138), but none of these precautions prevents him from falling overwhelmingly in love with madame de Tourvel. Whatever deliberate ambiguity he may put into his other letters, there is no reason to doubt the sincerity of the remark, 'croyez-moi, on n'est heureux que par l'amour', with which he ends his letter to Danceny (155). He does not need to introduce this idea in order to convince Danceny of the advantages to be derived from temporarily abandoning madame de Merteuil for Cécile, and his statement, 'je payerai de la moitié de ma vie le bonheur de pouvoir lui consacrer l'autre', seems both to foreshadow and to explain his death. Although Laclos does not say so explicitly, it is his despair at having sacrificed the one person who has brought him true happiness which makes him so ready to accept Danceny's challenge, and thus determined to avenge himself on madame de Merteuil before he dies. Yet this realisation that true happiness lies in the emotions comes too late to save Valmont. Like madame de Merteuil, he is 'hoist with his own petard', and destroyed because of his attempt to exploit human emotions while remaining immune to them himself. The letter which he sends to the Présidente, at madame de Merteuil's dictation—'Adieu, mon Ange, je t'ai prise avec plaisir, je te quitte sans regret: je te reviendrai peut-être. Ainsi va le monde. Ce n'est pas ma faute'(141) — epitomises the contrast which exists throughout the novel between form and subject matter. On the surface, all is eighteenth-century elegance and wit, and human emotions are amusing playthings. But in reality, the wit is murderous and the emotions violent enough to kill. On hearing the news of Valmont's death, the Présidente finally succumbs to the grief which overwhelmed her when she received this letter from him, and dies.

It is not only the ending of *Les Liaisons dangereuses* which can be used to support the view that it is a satirical novel composed by a sincere Rousseauist in order to stigmatise the immorality of the eighteenth-century French aristocracy and thus to defend, by implication, the values of marital fidelity which Rousseau had made fashionable. The incident which sets the plot in motion is extremely petty, and Valmont himself is made to comment upon the shallowness and monotony of his own life when he remarks to madame de Merteuil that their letters invariably come back to the same subject: 'toujours des femmes à avoir ou à perdre, et souvent tous les deux'(**76**). The Marxist critic Roger Vailland has argued that *Les Liaisons dangereuses* can be read as a kind of committed novel in which Laclos attacks the aristocracy whose privileges were such an obstacle to his own military career, and it is certainly tempting to interpret the novel in this way. Instead of fulfilling the traditional aristocratic functions of providing leadership in time of war and protecting his tenants in time of peace, Valmont does nothing but fritter away his talents on a series of vicious and pointless love affairs. Baudelaire himself drew attention to the social content of the novel when he commented that the Présidente was the only character belonging to the 'bourgeoisie' and not to the older, traditionally more powerful *noblesse d'épée*,[13] and her position may, in spite of the obviously high rank which she now occupies in society, have some similarities with Laclos's own. His family's patent of nobility was of very recent origin and his grandfather had actually been a tradesman. In so far as Rousseauism was a philosophy which appealed to the middle classes rather than to the aristocracy, Laclos's social situation would make him sympathise with the Présidente, and there is again a certain amount of external evidence to indicate that it was she rather than madame de Merteuil whom he regarded as his ideal woman. When his wife remarked in one of her letters to him in 1794 that 'la sensibilité est le trésor de tous, et qui n'est jamais de celui qui la possède', he regretted not having used her phrase, 'pour embellir le style de madame de Tourvel',[14] and the Présidente's virtue and simplicity of dress, as well as her spontaneity and deeply emotional nature, make her the perfect embodiment of the values that Laclos and Rousseau held most dear. Whether we look at the ending of the novel, with madame de Merteuil's complete failure to live up to her principles, at the more gradual destruction of Valmont's intellectualism by the emotions he had tried to suppress but which the Présidente brings to the surface, or at the relationship between Laclos's one novel and his more general philosophy of human relationships, the same conclusion emerges: *Les Liaisons dangereuses* is not a book which recommends what it describes, but a deliberate attack on the futility and wickedness of sexual immorality.

Such a reading in no way depends on evidence external to the text. Even if Laclos had been the worst of husbands and expressed nothing but scorn for Rousseau in his letters to his wife, the events in *Les Liaisons dangereuses* would still suggest that he was writing to satirise Valmont and madame de Merteuil, not to praise them. But the tone and atmosphere of a novel may often be at variance with the meaning to be read into its plot, just as the incidents in a man's life may sometimes appear to contradict what we think of as his personality. Laclos was undoubtedly, with his conscious mind, the best of family men and the most fervent of revolutionaries. But he was also, as his letters to his wife and other writings show, a very dull man when not writing *Les Liaisons dangereuses*. The letters to his wife are, as he rightly says, 'bavardage à la bonne amie de son cœur'.[15] The letters which madame de Tourvel receives from her husband were, as Valmont remarked, a 'mélange indigeste de détails de procès et de tirades d'amour conjugal'(**44**), and it is sobering to reflect how similar to the présidente de Tourvel Valmont's creator was in his own private life. If, in the final analysis, the gulf separating Laclos the novelist from Laclos the moralist and good family man is less wide than at first appears, the discrepancy is at least worth examining for any light which it may throw on two problems: how should *Les Liaisons dangereuses* be interpreted; and what is the relationship between an author and the books he writes?

Atmosphere and interpretation

This 'moral' interpretation is indeed more acceptable after we have finished the novel than while we are actually reading it. For all their wickedness, Valmont and madame de Merteuil fascinate the reader by their wit, charm and intelligence, and although it is difficult to share all of Saintsbury's scorn for the 'lacrimose, stoop-to-folly-and-ring-his-bosom madame de Tourvel',[16] she does begin by looking a little pale by the side of madame de Merteuil. When Valmont sticks to his principles in the face of great difficulties (**110**), having consciously entered into rivalry with God for the possession of madame de Tourvel—'J'aurai cette femme; je l'enlèverai au mari qui la profane; j'oserai la ravir au Dieu même qu'elle adore'(**16**)— and declared, in letter 23, 'Laissons le Braconnier obscur tuer à l'affût le cerf qu'il a surpris; le vrai Chasseur doit le forcer', he almost becomes the hero in the traditional sense of the word. André Malraux considered that Laclos's greatest originality lay in the creation of characters who acted, as Stendhal's or Dostoievski's heroes were to do in the following century, in accordance with a consistent philosophy of life,[17] and his remarks apply even more to madame de Merteuil than to Valmont. 'Mais moi, qu'ai-je de commun avec ces femmes inconsidérées?' she asks Valmont.

> Quand m'avez-vous vue m'écarter des règles que je me suis
> prescrites, et manquer à mes principes? je dis mes principes, et je
> le dis à dessein: car ils ne sont pas, comme ceux des autres
> femmes, donnés au hasard, reçus sans examen et suivis par
> habitude; ils sont le fruit de mes profondes réflexions; je les ai
> créés, et je puis dire que je suis mon ouvrage. (81)

The war which she has undertaken against the whole of the
male sex is a deliberate protest against the unjust disadvantages
which, in her view, a predominantly masculine society imposes
upon women, and at one point in this letter she comes close to
anticipating Figaro's challenge to Almaviva, in that:

> Quand je vous accorderais autant de talents qu'à nous, de
> combien encore ne devrions-nous pas vous surpasser, par la
> nécessité où nous sommes d'en faire un continuel usage.

sounds remarkably like:

> Qu'avez-vous fait pour tant de biens? vous vous êtes donné la
> peine de naître et rien de plus [...] tandis que moi, morbleu,
> perdu dans la foule obscure, il m'a fallu déployer plus de science
> et de calculs pour subsister seulement qu'on n'en a mis depuis
> cent ans à gouverner toutes les Espagnes... [18]

The feminist challenge is almost as strong here as it is when
Laclos declares, in his first essay on women's education, that
'on ne sort de l'esclavage que par une grande révolution'.[19]
Her self-portrait in letter 81 and Laclos's essays on women's
education are two sides of the same coin, and it is certainly
tempting to prefer madame de Merteuil's intensely rational
approach to Laclos's more sentimental plea for women's
rights, involving as it does the idealised portrait of a state of
nature where women are comfortably on their feet again, 'peu
de jours après l'enfantement'.[20] One does indeed wonder,
comparing *Les Liaisons dangereuses* to *Des femmes et de leur
éducation*, whether madame de Merteuil has not taken the
better part. She lives in a real world, has a full grasp of reality
and an intelligent understanding of other people, and does
attack male superiority in the one field where masculine
pretensions are both vulnerable and unjustified: that of sexual
activity. Indeed, her behaviour may even be defended by
reference to *Des femmes et de leur éducation* itself, for Laclos
suggests at one point in his essay that the only way in which a
woman can overcome male tyranny is by having 'l'adresse de
lier les mains à son maître et de commander à son tour'.[21] It is
only by considering another aspect of Rousseau's ideas, the
rehabilitation of marriage in *La Nouvelle Héloïse*—a book
which moved Laclos to tears when he read it at the age of

twenty and which remained his 'bible de sensibilité' throughout his life[22]—that madame de Merteuil can clearly be seen to be wrong in terms of the philosophy which Laclos himself adopted, and it is only on reflection, and after a fairly close study of the text, that the extent to which her feminism has turned sour can really be appreciated.

This ambiguity in Laclos's attitude towards madame de Merteuil recurs even more noticeably in his creation of Valmont, and there are a number of episodes in his biography which suggest that he would not have been averse to carrying out some of his hero's exploits himself. Thus a poem entitled *Le Bon Choix*,[23] published in 1779 three years before the appearance of *Les Liaisons dangereuses*, implies that Laclos did make the occasional though unsuccessful attempt to seduce certain ladies of his acquaintance, and even Roger Vailland, insistent though he is that Valmont is Laclos's class enemy, writes that Laclos created his hero out of a kind of wish-fulfilment, making him 'l'insolent qu'il aurait tant aimé être'.[24] Great though Laclos's devotion to his wife may have been, there is something odd about the fact that his son, Étienne-Fargeau, was born in 1784 and that Laclos did not marry Mlle Duperré until May 1786, and we know virtually nothing about his private life before his marriage.[25] There is certainly a tone of connivance in Laclos's account of Valmont's or madame de Merteuil's activities, and the conflict between his Rousseauist principles and the sympathy he felt for his characters comes out in the one aesthetic mistake that his novel contains. Why, it may well be asked, does he pile on the agony at the end of the book, and have madame de Merteuil disfigured by smallpox? She has already been sufficiently punished by the revelation of her true character to the society she has so long deceived, and it is made very clear throughout the novel that she depends absolutely, both socially and morally, on what other people think of her. That she should lose her lawsuit is just acceptable, since this is connected with her loss of reputation. But in spite of Laurent Versini's observation that two-thirds of the population in eighteenth-century France caught smallpox,[26] it is highly unlikely that madame de Merteuil should catch it at the very moment when she has just been socially disgraced. It is almost as if Laclos is over-compensating for the attraction which she exercised over him, and telling himself as well as his readers that she really is wicked enough to deserve every punishment. Dostoievski thought that he accepted the most authoritarian teaching of the Russian Orthodox Church, but he nevertheless made Ivan Karamazov, the atheist and the rebel, a far more interesting and convincing character than the saintly Alyosha.

Something rather similar may well have happened when Laclos created Valmont and madame de Merteuil, and it is probably because he put so much of his repressed or subconscious self into them that it is so difficult for us to condemn them while we are actually reading the novel. They appeal to that aspect of our own personality which, like Laclos himself, we feel we ought to suppress: the part which encourages us to see ourselves as totally in control of those situations where we normally depend most heavily on what other people think and feel. We close the book with a heightened recognition of why we ought to suppress this tendency, and an intense awareness of the harm we might do both to ourselves and to other people if we could always do what we wanted in our sexual or emotional life. But we are not convinced that either we or Laclos could ever succeed in altogether abolishing this tendency in human nature.

If Laclos were a thoroughgoing moralist in the Rousseauist tradition, or even if he were a socially committed writer anticipating in the novel the harm he attempted to do to the *ancien régime* once he was able to take part in politics, his book would not have this ambiguity. Madame de Tourvel would be unmistakably the heroine, while Valmont and madame de Merteuil would be as obviously unpleasant as Jane Murdstone or Uriah Heep. On the other hand, if Laclos had wholeheartedly endorsed madame de Merteuil's ambition to rule by stealth and humiliate by charm, and if he had been totally absorbed in his admiration for Valmont as the *arbiter elegantiarum* of eighteenth-century seduction, the smallpox that disfigures her and the duel in which he is killed would indeed have been nothing more than ironic comments on the extreme improbability of the punishments which normally overtake the wicked in most moralising novels. As it is, however, both Valmont and madame de Merteuil are also punished in a way logically connected with their earlier behaviour: if they had not tried to soar so high, they would not have fallen so low; if Valmont had not tried to seduce the Présidente, he would not have fallen in love with her; and if madame de Merteuil had not underestimated Valmont, she would not have pushed her luck too far by taking Danceny as her lover. It is partly this ambiguity which makes *Les Liaisons dangereuses* into a realistic novel, in the sense that it shows vice to be at one and the same time both very attractive and very harmful, and it may well have been this novel that Baudelaire had in mind when he wrote:

L'art est-il utile? Oui. Pourquoi? Parce qu'il est l'art. Y a-t-il un art pernicieux? Oui. C'est celui qui dérange les conditions de la ‾vie. Le vice est séduisant, il faut le peindre séduisant; mais il traîne avec lui des maladies et des douleurs morales singulières; il faut les décrire. Étudiez toutes les plaies comme un médecin qui fait son service dans un hôpital, et l'école du bon sens, l'école exclusivement morale, ne trouvera plus où mordre. Le crime est-il toujours châtié, la vertu gratifiée? Non; mais cependant, si votre roman, si votre drame est bien fait, il ne prendra envie à personne de violer les lois de la nature. La première condition nécessaire pour faire un art sain est la croyance à l'unité intégrale. Je défie qu'on me trouve un seul ouvrage d'imagination qui réunisse toutes les conditions du beau et qui soit un ouvrage pernicieux.[27]

Yet for all the intellectual fascination which the very ambiguity of *Les Liaisons dangereuses* has enabled it to exercise over so many readers, it would not deserve to rank among the best French novels—André Gide unhesitatingly placed it second, immediately after *La Chartreuse de Parme* [28] —if it did not possess an abundance of more purely literary qualities. It is these qualities which make it worth our while to find out whether it was written by a sincere disciple of Rousseau or an envious admirer of Valmont—or, as is most probable, by a man who was a mixture of both. At the same time, they offer the best answer to the problem of how the book should be interpreted.

Notes

(1)   Reference edition, p. 692. Versini's is much fuller than Maurice Allem's and contains all Laclos's surviving letters to his wife, as well as one (pp. 968-70) which she wrote him in October 1800, when he had gone back into the army, and which shows her to have shared all his views on marriage and children.

Laurent Versini also points out, in his note to letter 9 (p. 1190), that the action of the novel probably takes in the late summer, autumn and winter of 1768; or, possibly, 1769. Letter 9 refers to the 'mouvements de guerre' still taking place in Corsica, which had become a French possession on 15 May 1768. The resistance organised by Pascal Paoli ended with the battle of Ponte Novo on 8 May 1769, so it is just possible that Gercourt's regiment was still required to keep the peace as late as October of that year.

It is extremely unlikely that Laclos based his novel on an actual collection of letters between real people. The book is much too well structured for that, and real life does not produce the linguistic and emotional echoes and parallels which make *Les Liaisons dangereuses* such a continual delight to read. The thesis advanced in the book *Les Vrais Mémoires de Cécile de Volanges, rectification et suite aux 'Liaisons dangereuses'*, published in 1926 by an ingenious bibliophile called Lucas de Peslouan, as well as in another book mentioned on p. 1259 of the Pléiade reference edition, R. Peter's *La Dame aux repentirs, l'inspiratrice des 'Liaisons dangereuses'*, has to be seen as the French equivalent of speculations in the journals of *The Sherlock Holmes Society* as to whether the great man went to Oxford or to Cambridge. The mention of the events in Corsica nevertheless suggests that Laclos did mean his readers to situate the action of his novel fairly precisely at the beginning of the 1770s. The clear allusions to the 1780s in the text of Christopher Hampton's play *Les Liaisons dangereuses* are thus justified more by the general atmosphere of the novel than by the actual text.

(2)   Quoted in A. and Y. Delmas, *A la recherche des 'Liaisons dangereuses'* (Mercure de France, 1964), p. 60.

(3)   Delmas, *op. cit.*, p. 60.

(4)   *Idem* , p. 62.

(5)   George Saintsbury, *A History of the French Novel to the Close of the Nineteenth Century* (Macmillan and Co., 1917), preface, p. xiv.

(6)   Martin Turnell, *The Novel in France* (Hamish Hamilton, 1950), p. viii.

(7)   'Le Mariage de Laclos', *Revue d'Histoire Littéraire de la France*, LXIV (1964), 60-72 [p. 60].

(8)   Émile Dard, *Le Général Choderlos de Laclos, auteur des 'Liaisons dangereuses', 1741–1803* (Perrin et Cie, 1905), p. 450.

(9)   Quoted in the Allem edition, p. 710.

(10) 'Notes sur *Les Liaisons dangereuses*', in *Œuvres complètes*, ed. C. Pichois (NRF Gallimard, 'Bibliothèque de la Pléiade', 1975-1976), t. II, pp. 66-75 [p. 68].

(11) La Harpe's judgment is in the Allem edition, pp. 703-704.

(12) Rather quickly, since Valmont first sleeps with her on 1 October (**96**), and letter 115 is dated 19 October. The literally-minded reader, invited by the careful construction of the novel to think of the events as having actually happened, wonders just exactly how Valmont knows. Cécile cannot have told him in so many words, since letter 140, dated 22 November, describing her miscarriage, states quite specifically that she herself did not even realise that she was pregnant. Cécile's lack of awareness of the fact that one of the first signs of pregnancy is an interruption in the menstrual cycle is yet another indication of how inadequate her general education has been, both in her convent and at the hands of her mother. Perhaps one is to imagine Valmont carrying out the instructions referred to in letter 110 ('je lui ai tout appris, jusqu'aux complaisances; je n'ai excepté que les précautions') to the point of asking Cécile when her last period was, but carefully abstaining from explaining to her the real import of his question. This would fit in with his remark in letter 115: 'j'attends une seconde époque pour confirmer mon espoir', and the phrase in letter 140—'pour des raisons que vous devinerez, ou que vous ne devinerez pas, Mme de Tourvel ne m'occupait plus depuis quelques jours'—shows a Valmont fully aware of what was happening to the menstrual cycle of his various mistresses.

(13) 'Notes sur *Les Liaisons dangereuses*', p. 71. It would perhaps be less extravagant to situate her in the *noblesse de robe*

(14) Reference edition, p. 799, letter of 6 May 1794, dated by Laclos as *17 floréal, an s[econ]d de la Rép[ublique] une et indiv[isible]*.

This was one of the many letters which Laclos wrote to his wife while imprisoned in the gaol at Picpus, and it may be that his insistence on using the new revolutionary calendar, running from 21 September 1792 (*1 vendémiaire, an premier de la République une et indivisible*), owes something to his knowledge that his letters risked being intercepted and read for signs of possible disloyalty to the new régime. Sensibly enough, he does not refer to Robespierre, Couthon and Saint-Just as 'traitors' until 30 July 1794, twenty days after they had been executed as a result of losing power on the *9 thermidor, an II de la République*. Later on he refers in glowing terms to Bonaparte, describing him on 10 July 1800, six months after he had taken power by the coup d'état of the *18 brumaire, an VIII de la République* (9 November 1799) as 'l'Immortel Général'(p. 916), whose presence on the battlefield is worth an additional 30,000 men (p. 1004, 28 November 1800, *7 frimaire an IX de la Rép[ublique] française une et indivisible*).

Laclos's letters contain another charming compliment to his wife. When she complained that she was getting fat, he wrote to her from Milan on 14 April 1800 (p. 1068, *24 germinal, an IX*) that the more there was of her, the better.

(15) *Lettres inédites* (Mercure de France, 1904), p. 164.

(16) Saintsbury, *op. cit.*, p. xiv. The spelling is Saintsbury's own.

(17)   See his *Scènes choisies* (Gallimard, 1946), pp. 334-43.

(18)   Beaumarchais, *Le Mariage de Figaro,* Act V, scene 3.

(19)   Reference edition, *Des femmes et de leur éducation,* p. 391.

(20)   *Idem,* p. 395.

(21)   Dard, *op. cit.,* p. 17.

(22)   *Idem,* p. 433.

(23)   See reference edition, pp. 555-6.

(24)   Roger Vailland, *Laclos par lui-même* (Éditions du Seuil, 1959), p. 26.

(25)   See Dard, *op. cit.,* pp. 109 and 160. For an alternative and more probable interpretation of Laclos's marriage, arguing that he delayed marrying Marie-Soulange only because of problems over her dowry, with no need to use Valmont's technique on a lady who, by eighteenth-century standards, was—at twenty-three—almost on the shelf when he met her, see Pomeau, *loc. cit.*
    The evidence in favour of a Laclos who was highly moral in his private life is nevertheless overwhelming, especially after his marriage. He was a devoted but worried father, understandably anxious to provide for his wife and children at a very troubled period in French history. Initially, he wanted his son Étienne to learn about agriculture, and his daughter to acquaint herself with the eighteenth-century equivalent of office practice and book-keeping. Later, after he had succeeded in placing Étienne as a diplomatic attaché with the duc de La Rochefoucauld, he was disappointed by the young man's slowness in learning German, as well as by his appalling spelling. Some time in April 1800, this led to the humiliation for Laclos of having monsieur de La Rochefoucauld ask him: 'Comment est-il possible qu'un fils de monsieur de Laclos mette l'orthographe comme une cuisinière?'
    Laclos's last surviving letter (p. 1132) is a dignified appeal to Bonaparte to do something for his wife and children, and the First Consul obliged. Madame de Laclos received a pension of 1,000 francs a year (the average wage for a working man in Paris, which was just under a franc a day in the 1780s). In March 1782, Laclos had received 1,600 livres (=francs) on the signature of the contract for *Les Liaisons dangereuses,* and in 1788, when he became secretary to the duc d'Orléans, his salary was 6,000 francs a year. After Laclos's death, Étienne was accepted as a cadet at the École Militaire and Charles, then nine years old, as a pupil at a military academy. Charles married, and in 1849, after the death of her husband in 1844, his widow gave the manuscript of *Les Liaisons dangereuses* to the Bibliothèque Nationale.

(26)   Versini, *Laclos et la tradition. Essai sur les sources et la technique des 'Liaisons dangereuses'* (Klincksieck, 1968), p. 221.

(27)   *Les Drames et les Romans honnêtes, Œuvres complètes,* t. II, p. 41.

(28)   Quoted by Turnell, *op. cit.,* p. viii.

Chapter Two

The Aesthetic Solution

Composition

Whenever Laclos's regiment was inspected, during his long years of service under the *ancien régime,* he received excellent reports for his skill as an artillery officer, and he is also credited with having made a series of experiments that led to the replacement of the solid cannon ball with the explosive shell.[1] All the details of his novel fit together with an economy and elegance which bear witness to his prowess in mathematics and strategy, and this economy is particularly noticeable in the complete absence of superfluous characters. Thus madame de Volanges, by arranging for Cécile to marry Gercourt, does much more than provide the initial impulse which sets the plot going. By not even giving her daughter the opportunity to meet her fiancé, and allowing her to discover from madame de Merteuil the appalling fact that Gercourt is thirty-six years old (**39**), she is making it virtually certain that Cécile will rebel against the marriage arranged for her, will be attracted to Danceny, and will be all the more vulnerable to the influence of madame de Merteuil. This influence is decisive in handing Cécile completely over to Valmont at a critical moment in the plot (**105**), and it is the action of the novel itself rather than any sermons from the author which drives home one of the main ideas which Laclos shares with Rousseau: parents should take a much closer and more personal interest in educating their children, and beware of exposing them to the possibly self-interested advice of strangers. This failure of madame de Volanges to look after her daughter properly is paralleled by the deliberately bad education which Valmont gives her— 'dans ce court intervalle, l'écolière est devenue presque aussi savante que le maître'(**110**)—and it is significant that one of the few definite claims which Laclos makes for the social usefulness of *Les Liaisons dangereuses* lies in the portrait which it gives of the dangers threatening a mother, 'qui souffre qu'un autre qu'elle ait la confiance de sa fille'.[2]

Madame de Volanges is also used as an involuntary agent to

18

keep the plot moving and as an example of how inadequate the traditional attitudes become in any complex situation. Laclos must surely have intended his readers to link her disastrous interventions in the plot with the extreme conventionality of her ideas, and there is an element of symbolism in the fact that it is her attempts to warn the Présidente against Valmont which ultimately decide him to fall in with madame de Merteuil's plan. From the moment that Valmont discovers that it is this 'infernale mégère' who has been reinforcing madame de Tourvel's resistance (**44**), Cécile's downfall is virtually assured, and it is both significant and ironic that when madame de Volanges discovers her daughter's affair with Danceny, she should try to protect her by taking her to the very château where Valmont will seduce her (**63**). Laclos makes it quite clear in letter 98 that madame de Volanges's original decision to marry Cécile to Gercourt was motivated primarily by snobbery, and this vanity not only serves the purpose of emphasising yet again the dangers of following the conventions of society rather than the promptings of the heart; it also fits very neatly into the characterisation of the novel by enabling the reader to see just how skilfully madame de Merteuil can overcome a sudden obstacle to one of her plans.

Thus when Cécile bursts into tears on the morning after she has been seduced by Valmont (**98**), her mother immediately thinks that she is crying over her separation from Danceny, and is so moved that she is on the point of breaking her word to Gercourt and allowing Cécile to marry the man she loves. This, of course, is the very last thing that madame de Merteuil wants to happen, and she uses the most impeccably conservative and authoritarian arguments to convince madame de Volanges that she should not sacrifice her daughter's long-term happiness to any such romantic whim (**104**). This letter is important partly because it completes the picture of madame de Volanges as a well-meaning but foolish woman, and reveals how thoroughly madame de Merteuil can betray all those who trust her; but it is also an excellent illustration of how Laclos never contents himself, as lesser novelists do, with simply telling his readers how intelligent his main characters are. He actually shows them being intelligent in the letters they write and the plans they carry out, and *Les Liaisons dangereuses*, in this respect, provides something of the same intellectual pleasure as a well-constructed *comédie d'intrigue* or a cleverly planned detective story. However, Laclos does much more than simply make the pieces fit perfectly together. He combines planning with psychological analysis, and the use which he makes of Valmont's aged aunt, madame de Rosemonde, is a particularly good example of the complex but extremely coherent pattern into which he weaves the different characters, ideas and events in *Les Liaisons dangereuses*.

Like madame de Volanges, madame de Rosemonde could have very easily remained a fairly superfluous character on the edge of the plot, simply the person at whose country house Valmont first meets the Présidente. However, when madame de Tourvel starts to grow fonder of Valmont, she needs a more indulgent *confidente* than madame de Volanges, and Valmont's aunt is there quite naturally to fulfil the role. Madame de Tourvel's surrender is made psychologically more probable by the information which madame de Rosemonde gives her about Valmont's supposed illness and imminent conversion (**122**), and there is again considerable irony in the fact that it should be madame de Rosemonde who plays so important a part in enabling Valmont finally to seduce the Présidente. She is the person who will feel most grief when this seduction brings death to them both, and yet it is she who makes it possible. Again, like madame de Volanges, madame de Rosemonde is a character who represents official morality, but in her case Laclos underlines its inadequacy in a different and possibly more significant way. Whereas madame de Volanges has impeccable principles but is too unperceptive to realise what is going on, madame de Rosemonde has a fairly shrewd idea of how people behave but lacks any firm moral standards by which to judge them. Her advice to madame de Tourvel is tinged with the gentle scepticism about official values that characterises all societies which have mellowed with age and are ripe for destruction. The need for new values is thus implicit in the failure of both madame de Volanges and madame de Rosemonde to protect those they love, and in this respect Laclos's technique as a novelist is a good illustration of the views on marriage and society which he expressed in his essays on women's education and seems to have observed in his own life.

According to Count Alexandre de Tilly, who knew Laclos when the novelist was working in London for Philippe d'Orléans during the early years of the Revolution, much of the material for *Les Liaisons dangereuses* came from incidents which Laclos himself had heard about during his army career. He had, apparently, based his creation of madame de Merteuil on a lady in Grenoble, 'une marquise de L.T.D.P.M. dont toute la ville racontait des traits dignes des jours des Impératrices Romaines les plus insatiables',[3] and critics have naturally spent much time and energy in trying to find out who this Marquise really was. Whether she actually existed at all, however, is less important than what Laclos made of her: he transposed her purely sexual appetites into the almost abstract desire for power which gives madame de Merteuil her interest and originality. Laclos's ability to use his sources for primarily psychological effects is also visible in another aspect of the novel, for Tilly also reports him as saying that he had incorporated into *Les Liaisons dangereuses* 'quelques petites historiettes [...] assez piquantes' which he had overheard in his youth. The Prévan episode and Valmont's adventures with Émilie or the vicomtesse de M*** are obviously anecdotes of this sort, and provide a general background which makes the basic intrigue of the novel seem more probable. However, this is by no means their most important function, for Laclos also uses them to illustrate one of the main psychological themes in his novel, the rivalry between madame de Merteuil and Valmont. Thus it is highly significant that Valmont puts off congratulating madame de Merteuil on her triumph over Prévan until has has restored his own prestige by seducing Cécile, and his reluctance is linked with the broader issue of the sex war by his mention of his long-standing conviction 'que quand il n'y avait plus que des louanges à donner à une femme, on pouvait s'en reposer sur elle, et s'occuper d'autre chose'(**96**).

Where even the better eighteenth-century novelists content themselves with a series of anecdotes linked together by an extremely tenuous central thread—the narrator in Prévost's *Mémoires d'un homme de qualité* reproducing des Grieux's account of his passion for Manon Lescaut, or Marivaux's Marianne, actress and narrator through eleven episodic volumes—Laclos introduces into the novel something of the concern for psychological relevance which had earlier characterised classical tragedy, and these 'petites historiettes' are not only used to show how Valmont and madame de Merteuil are perpetually trying to score points off one another. They are also highly relevant to the seduction of the Présidente by Valmont and the genuine love affair which arises accidently from this. Émilie and the vicomtesse de M*** are women with whom Valmont tries to forget how seriously he is in love with madame de Tourvel, and his second encounter with Émilie, when the Présidente sees them together in his carriage and is heartbroken at this public spectacle of her betrayal, is used by Laclos to produce one of his best narrative effects. It anticipates in farce what will later happen tragically, for it is a similar but more subtle humiliation which madame de Merteuil finally succeeds in imposing upon the Présidente through Valmont's cooperation. Moreover, it is through what is actually presented in the text as one of these anecdotes—'Un homme de ma connaissance s'était empêtré, comme vous, d'une femme qui lui faisait peu d'honneur'

(**141**)—that madame de Merteuil kills the love between
Valmont and the Présidente, and the weapon which she chooses
is fully in keeping with the world of promiscuity and
libertinage that these 'petites historiettes' represent. Valmont
had almost escaped from this world by falling genuinely in
love, and it is in the conflict between the world of *sensibilité*
incarnated in the Présidente and the world of intellectualised
sex reflected in madame de Merteuil that the fundamental
balance of the novel is to be found.

Like his exploitation of these anecdotes, Laclos's use of the
epistolary form is also well subordinated to his preoccupation
with psychological analysis, and it is this subordination which
provides a particularly convincing reply to La Harpe's
objection that it is absurd for madame de Merteuil to write
'toutes les horreurs imaginables' about herself in her letters to
Valmont.[4] As Laurent Versini observes in a slightly different
context, 'la jouissance dans *Les Liaisons dangereuses* ne
consiste pas tant à faire le mal qu'à le dire',[5] and madame de
Merteuil needs Valmont as a vain woman needs her looking-
glass and her admirers. If he did not know that she had
defeated Prévan, she would find her victory scarcely worth
having; and Valmont's own seduction of Cécile and the
Présidente would be almost valueless in his own eyes if
madame de Merteuil were not to recognise his achievements. It
is therefore essential that they communicate with each other,
and there are excellent psychological reasons why they should
do so only by letter. Had Valmont kept his promise to call
upon madame de Merteuil (**47**; **51**), or had the Marquise
responded to his suggestion that they meet at the house of the
maréchale de *** (**66**; **70**), the crisis in their relationship
would have had to be settled one way or the other. However,
neither can allow this to happen while the question of the
Présidente's seduction still hangs in the balance, and this
failure to keep their appointments is clearly a deliberate move
in their contest for supremacy. Valmont meets madame de
Merteuil only once, when he surprises her with Danceny
(**151**), and this meeting immediately produces the quarrel
which ends the book. It thereby shows, in retrospect, how
important their physical separation has been on a deeper,
symbolic level, and how right Laclos is to keep them apart
until then.

In the peak year of 1787, fourteen epistolary novels were
published in France alone,[6] but *Les Liaisons dangereuses* is not
a novel which simply happens to be in the letter form because
this was the convention. In the same way that Valmont and
madame de Merteuil can satisfy their vanity only by

exchanging letters, the plot works itself out only because the characters write to one another. As has already been observed, it is because he finds madame de Volanges's letters to the Présidente that Valmont decides to seduce Cécile (44), and because he intercepts madame de Tourvel's letters to madame de Rosemonde (115) that he knows the time is ripe for his final attack. It is also because the Présidente gives Valmont permission to write to her that the reader can see how he puts into practice his intention of gradually forcing her from one position to another, until she is almost compelled to surrender merely because of the sense of obligation which he has managed to give her. Thus the Présidente's detailed reproaches to Valmont in letter 78 show how well the strategy which he describes in letter 23 is working out, and it is a letter that breaks off their affair just as it was a series of letters which prepared her seduction. It is because madame de Merteuil has written so much about herself that she is so irretrievably ruined, for without the letters that he has so carefully retained, Valmont would have been able to prove little against her. The idea that the présidente de Tourvel always remains on a totally different plane from Valmont and madame de Merteuil is again suggested by a device inseparable from the fact that *Les Liaisons dangereuses* is an epistolary novel, for Valmont never shows the Marquise the love letters which she is convinced the Présidente must be sending him after he has seduced her—'ou je me trompe, ou la tendre dévote doit beaucoup écrire' (131)—and which he was to have shown her as a proof both of his triumph over madame de Tourvel and his continued preference for madame de Merteuil (20; 131). This is a particularly interesting feature of his technique, since it shows Laclos as deliberately inviting the reader to speculate freely on what interpretation should be given to certain events. Thus it may well be that, for once, madame de Merteuil is wrong, and has completely failed to understand what kind of a woman the Présidente is. If that is so, and madame de Tourvel never writes a passionate love letter to Valmont, then his seduction of her is complete only in a physical and emotional manner. He never succeeds in bringing her down to the social and intellectual level on which he lives with madame de Merteuil, and where it is considered normal for a love affair to be a pretext for letter writing. Another possibility, however, is that madame de Tourvel does write to Valmont, but that he chooses not to forward her letters to madame de Merteuil. If so, then the suggestion is that Valmont finally prefers the Présidente to madame de Merteuil and consciously refuses to bring her down to the same level as the other women he has had.

Laclos is by no means the only novelist to leave space for

the reader's imagination to work—*did* Becky Sharp become Lord Steyne's mistress; what *was* the relationship between Annette Forsyte and Prosper Profond?—but the epistolary form is especially suited to creating the illusion that the characters in a novel enjoy an independent existence outside the words printed on the page.[7] Laclos had his tongue only half in his cheek when he warned the reader in the *Préface du rédacteur* that he had been allowed to omit everything from the original correspondence that was not essential 'soit à l'intelligence des événements, soit au développement des caractères',[8] and there is also matter for considerable speculation in the fact that Valmont himself never refers to madame de Merteuil's insistence that he send her the Présidente's love letters. The very omissions which Laclos is careful to make invite the reader to use his imagination to fill in the gaps which exist even in the most articulate of people between what they say and what they feel, and encourage him in the pleasant illusion that the characters in the book do exist outside the printed page.

While Laclos is never so blatantly self-conscious a novelist as the Gide of *Les Faux-Monnayeurs* or the Huxley of *Point Counter Point*, he does nevertheless provide a comment, in the excellent advice which madame de Merteuil gives to Cécile Volanges, on how he himself uses the epistolary form. 'Vous voyez bien', she tells her, 'que, quand vous écrivez à quelqu'un, c'est pour lui et non pas pour vous: vous devez donc moins chercher à lui dire ce que vous pensez, que ce qui lui plaît davantage'(105). While her remark applies very well to the technique which she herself uses on madame de Volanges or which Valmont employs on père Anselme (120), it also offers an excellent comment on Laclos's own continual awareness of how his reader is going to react to the letters in *Les Liaisons dangereuses*. Although the marquise de Merteuil and Valmont always do in fact write their letters for themselves in the sense that they always have some ulterior motive, and are interested in other people's preferences only in so far as these provide an opening for flattery, Laclos never forgets that the same letter can take on a very different meaning according to the person reading it and the context in which it is read. It is again on the reader's imagination that he relies for some of the best effects which he derives from this advantage of the epistolary form, and *Les Liaisons dangereuses* is a novel which must be read with the same kind of sustained attention and awareness of ambiguity which are normally reserved for difficult poetry.

The most obvious example of Laclos's use of ambiguity is

letter 48, which the Présidente can read as a romantic declaration of love but whose real function is to show madame de Merteuil—and the reader—how witty Valmont can be. Perhaps significantly for Laclos's general reputation, it is probably the best known letter in *Les Liaisons dangereuses*, and it is certainly very amusing. It is not, however, the best example of the more subtle effects which Laclos can draw from the different ways in which the same letter can be read. When madame de Volanges, for example, describes Cécile's distress and considers whether she ought still to insist on the marriage with Gercourt (**98**) madame de Merteuil reads the letter from her own very privileged point of view. She knows that Cécile has been crying because Valmont has just seduced her, and can thus give a quite unintended meaning to madame de Volanges's phrase about 'le choix qu'il veut faire de la mère de ses enfants'. Laclos never forgets the reader looking over the shoulder of the person to whom the letter is officially addressed, and his use of the different ways in which the same letter can be read becomes increasingly subtle and complex as the tension rises towards the end of the novel. In letter 122, for example, we read madame de Rosemonde's account of Valmont's illness through the Présidente's eyes, and our knowledge of the trust which she places in Valmont's aunt enables us to understand how deeply she is affected. The most dramatic effects, however, are reserved for letters 126 and 128, and the contrast between these two letters is perhaps the most original use of the epistolary technique in the whole book. We know, when we first read letter 126, that the Présidente is now Valmont's mistress, and therefore imagine her anguish as each warning from madame de Rosemonde twists the knife in the wound. But letter 128 shows us how thoroughly Laclos had led us up the garden path, for we learn from it that nothing can now affect madame de Tourvel's happiness so long as she has Valmont's love. Instead of merely telling us that the Présidente loves Valmont, Laclos shows us the intensity of this love by the ease with which she overcomes the remorse which we have previously been made to imagine as quite overwhelming.

Closely linked with this very effective use of the epistolary technique is Laclos's ability to show each event from a number of different angles. Thus, in addition to the mixture of intellectual pleasure and sexual jealousy which we imagine madame de Merteuil to feel as she reads Valmont's account of how he seduces Cécile (**96**), we have Cécile's naïvely sensuous version of the same events (**97**), and madame de Volanges's total misunderstanding of the whole situation (**98**). When madame de Volanges, as a typically respectable woman, is quite taken in by madame de Merteuil's official account of her adventure with Prévan (87), Laclos underlines how successful a hypocrite the Marquise can be. At the same time, he offers additional amusement to the reader by the contrast with the true version that madame de Merteuil sends to Valmont (85). Sartre's much later contention that 'la théorie de la relativité s'applique intégralement à l'univers romanesque et, dans un vrai roman, non plus que dans le monde d'Einstein, il n'y a de place pour un observateur privilégié' [9] applies admirably to Laclos's technique of narration, for not even Valmont or madame de Merteuil has enough knowledge to act the omniscient narrator. It is always the reader who draws the threads together, and Laclos is especially skilful in giving him the illusion that he does so as a result of his own intelligence and never because the author has imposed a particular interpretation. Those aspects of the plot and characterisation of *Les Liaisons dangereuses* over which Laclos deliberately leaves a shadow of obscurity also recall Sartre's insistence on the need for the author to respect his reader's freedom, and one of them is all the more intriguing since it concerns the most intelligent and self-conscious person in the book. Does madame de Merteuil carry her hostility towards Valmont to the extent of encouraging madame de Volanges to warn the Présidente against him? Laclos does no more than hint, but madame de Merteuil is suspiciously friendly with madame de Volanges in the first part of the novel and madame de Volanges suspiciously well-informed about Valmont's earlier career. If madame de Merteuil is behaving in this way, then it may mean either that she is more jealous of Valmont than she dare admit even to herself, or that she is actually in love with him herself and prepared to use every means to keep him away from a person whom she has already identified as her only really dangerous rival. Laclos refuses to do more than suggest what madame de Merteuil is doing and why, and this recognition that the novelist himself, like his characters, has only a limited knowledge of events fits in perfectly with the subjectivity implicit in the different styles used in the novel.

Thus each character is given his or her own language, and is immediately recognisable because of it. Madame de Rosemonde, as befits a more or less permanent invalid, falls naturally into a medical vocabulary in her letters to madame de Tourvel (126, 130), and the ideas which she expresses are wholly in keeping with what the marquise de Merteuil shrewdly forecasts will be the tolerance stemming from her old age and long reflexions on human weakness (123). Cécile is completely unable to find any descriptive term other than 'bien', and in letter 75 it occurs nine times. When madame de

Merteuil ventures a criticism, she replies in characteristic style that 'Danceny trouve mes lettres bien comme elles sont'(**109**), and her immaturity is also underlined by the fact that other people have to write her letters for her. Her complete lack of control over her own fate is thus reflected in the very technique of the novel, and it is significant that Danceny resembles her in needing other people to tell him what to say (**64; 66**) as well as what to do (**155**). Laclos needs to include only the shortest letter from Gercourt to depict him as a pompous snob (**111**), while the reply which le père Anselme sends to Valmont keeps a perfect balance between spiritual concern and social flattery (**122**). It is true that when Azolan, Valmont's manservant, tells his master that the Présidente is reading a book called *Clarisse* and adds 'J'écris bien comme il y a: Monsieur saura peut-être ce que c'est'(**107**),[10] Laclos does seem to be showing the limitations of one particular viewpoint in a rather obvious way. Nevertheless, he redeems himself in the very same letter by a realistic touch which neatly emphasises one of the novel's main social themes. Although normally prepared to do anything for his master, Azolan does hope that he will not be required to enter the Présidente's service and 'porter la livrée, et encore une livrée de Robe, après avoir eu l'honneur d'être Chasseur de Monsieur'. Neither is it only Azolan's acute awareness of class distinctions which shows how different her social world is from that of Valmont or madame de Merteuil. Her position as a member of the legal nobility is clearly reflected by the vocabulary she uses, for when she asks 'Quel compte avons-nous à demander à celui qui ne nous doit rien?' and remarks of Valmont that: 'Le Dieu qui l'a formé devait chérir son ouvrage. Il n'avait point créé cet être charmant pour n'en faire qu'un réprouvé' (**124**), her ideas and turn of phrase have a markedly Jansenistic tone. It was among the *noblesse de robe* that this heresy always enjoyed its greatest popularity, and as if to underline both her passionate nature and the familiarity which her membership of this class would have given her with the Jansenist tradition, Laclos twice makes her express ideas which are virtual paraphrases of lines from *Phèdre*. 'Je m'égare encore dans des vœux criminels'(**102**) is an alexandrine which recalls Phèdre's 'Où laissé-je égarer mes vœux et mon esprit?'(l. 180), and her reluctance to name Valmont again recalls Phèdre's refusal to pronounce the name of Hippolyte.

If the aim of art is always to hide art, then the visible excellence of Laclos's technique might at first sight appear a defect, an indication that *Les Liaisons dangereuses* is too mechanically contrived to possess that inner, organic unity which is said to characterise great literature. Critics who accept Flaubert's idea that 'les chefs d'œuvre sont bêtes, ils ont la mine tranquille des grands animaux' tend to disparage works which are so obviously the product of human intelligence as *Les Liaisons dangereuses,* and it could be argued that Laclos is too clever—and his basic subject matter too unpleasant—for his novel to have the universal appeal of *Anna Karenina* or *Great Expectations.* It should be remembered, however, that for all his sympathy with Rousseau's ideas, Laclos was writing in the classical and not the romantic tradition. In particular, he was writing for a public which had been accustomed by the tradition of the *salons* to appreciate the finer points of literary composition, and which in no way accepted the view that the imaginative writer should hide his intelligence. Laclos was certainly too much of a gentleman to flaunt his learning, and his technique of narration is always subordinated to his analysis of character. Moreover, in this analysis, he uses the very qualities of wit and elegance which characterise *salon* literature in order to undermine the admiration which we initially feel for his brilliant hero and heroine, and reinforce the moral and social values which lie behind his condemnation of them.

Language

At first sight, Valmont and madame de Merteuil seem to be just as much in control of their language as they are of themselves and of the other people with whom they come into contact. When Valmont is writing to the Présidente, or the marquise de Merteuil to madame de Volanges or Cécile, each observes madame de Merteuil's own injunction to concentrate on the person who is going to receive their letter. They never startle their intended victim by an excessive display of intelligence, but reserve their wit for their private duel. When Valmont uses Émilie as a writing desk (**48**), he is aiming far more at madame de Merteuil than at the Présidente, and Laclos clearly indicates this by Valmont's feeble explanation of why madame de Merteuil should seal and post it (**45**). It is again significant that she no more congratulates him on his wit than he praises the skill with which she handles Prévan (**96**), and it is the implications of this refusal which suggest how the critical dilemma of *Les Liaisons dangereuses*—is it an attack on Valmont and madame de Merteuil or a glorification of their exploits?—can best be resolved. Both Valmont and madame de Merteuil have made the fundamental mistake of deciding to devote all their talents to ensuring that other people are constantly compelled to admire them. In Sartrian terms, they exist only 'pour autrui', Valmont's description of society as 'le grand théâtre'(70) has an especial meaning in this context. Like his description of himself as the 'héros d'un drame'(21), and like madame de Merteuil's repetition of 'le grand théâtre'(81) or the frequency of her visits to the theatre, it suggests that both he and the Marquise really live only for the applause which their exploits can evoke. Their quite genuine superiority has also led them to consider each other as the only audience whose applause is worth having, so that they depend upon each other for praise which they are both equally reluctant to give. Because they are physically separated, and because they live in a society which places the highest value on language, they fight a battle in which every epigram is a missile. Paradoxically, however, the very language which they use turns against them. It is by their own wit that they are undone, and it is because they do not really understand the language on which they so pride themselves that their failure is so absolute.

The very real control which Laclos has over his characters is most obvious in the fact that they are never finally allowed, for all the freedom which they seem to enjoy, to be witty purely on their own account. Their wit is constantly subordinated to his analysis of them. Madame de Merteuil's observation that 'on acquiert rarement les qualités dont on peut se passer'(81) is as good as anything in La Rochefoucauld, but is not an indication that, like Galatea or Unamuno's Augusto Pérez, she has escaped from her creator. It takes on its full significance only in the context of the self-assertive feminism which is, in a way, her tragic flaw, for she would neither make this remark nor behave as she does if she were not constantly striving to compete with everyone she encounters. It is true that she nearly always wins in her verbal exchanges with Valmont. When he complacently quotes the comtesse de ***'s remark that her husband 'a le plus beau bois du monde, qu'il conserve soigneusement pour ses amis'(59), her question 'Cet homme est donc l'ami de tout le monde?'(63) neatly and effectively pricks the bubble of his self-esteem. Later she will pick up his self-pitying 'ce n'est pas ma faute' (138)—itself an echo of her earlier phrase (106)—and use it against both him and the Présidente (141; 145), and for most of the time she says exactly what she means and does precisely as she wants. It is only when events begin to move beyond her and Valmont's control that the language which they have used so skilfully earlier in the novel turns against them, and that we realise how she too lacks some essential qualities.

Laclos himself noted in his preface that almost all the feelings expressed in *Les Liaisons dangereuses* are 'feints et dissimulés', and madame de Merteuil's letters are especially rich in a deliberate and highly entertaining ambiguity which stems directly from the fact that she consciously chooses to betray everyone with whom she comes into contact. When she describes Cécile to madame de Volanges as 'un enfant né de vous, et dont l'éducation modeste et pure n'a pu que fortifier l'heureux naturel'(**104**), we remember her earlier comment to Valmont about Cécile's 'fausseté naturelle'(**38**), recall her remark that she herself at fifteen, 'n'ayant jamais été au couvent', knew nothing at all about sexual matters (**81**), and smile appreciatively at the accuracy of her wit, while perhaps recognising an inconsistency in Laclos's criticism of convent education.[11] It is when things go wrong that her wit turns against her, and that her earlier remark about Danceny—'Oh! l'on peut se brouiller avec celui-là; les raccommodements ne sont pas dangereux' (**54**)—takes on quite a different meaning, for it is precisely Valmont's reconciliation (*raccommodement*) with Danceny immediately after the duel that brings about her disgrace. Similarly, when Valmont himself writes: 'madame de Tourvel m'a rendu les charmantes illusions de la jeunesse'(**6**), he thinks that such illusions exist only for his delight. However, when the Présidente makes him look like a novice in affairs of the heart (**99**; **100**), his words take on a different meaning and one whose full importance is revealed only when he discovers that he loves her with all the passion and despair of youth.

It is in this use of dramatic irony that Laclos's language and technique of narration reinforce the highly moral reading which can be given to what actually happens in *Les Liaisons dangereuses*. Valmont and madame de Merteuil have devoted their whole lives to analysing their own and other people's reactions, and yet in the last resort they can neither control what they do nor understand what they say. If neither of them falls quite to the level of Cécile Volanges, who writes to her beloved Danceny, at Valmont's dictation, that the latter 'fait tout comme vous feriez vous-même'(**117**), they are just as much the helpless puppets of their own emotions as Cécile is the toy which they intend to break after they have finished playing with it. In letter 21, for example, Valmont offers a most perceptive account of the emotional pleasures procured by self-conscious charity. Yet for all the critique of Rousseau that this description implies, it is sensibility which triumphs in the end. Valmont is finally obliged to have recourse to the typically Rousseauist device of an outburst of tears and a threat of suicide in order to seduce the Présidente (**125**), and it is only by the purest accident that he pronounces the word 'bonheur' which makes her his mistress in the fullest sense of the word. Valmont may comment shrewdly on other people's behaviour, as when he explains how Prévan felt encouraged when *les inséparables* accepted him into their circle—'Il savait assez que les gens heureux ne sont pas d'un accès si facile' (**79**)—but he quite fails to understand the woman he loves. Even after he has sent the Présidente the letter which madame de Merteuil virtually dictates to him, he still thinks that she might take him back (**141; 142; 154**). While still allowing them to be very much wittier than the normal sum of humanity, Laclos manœuvres Valmont and madame de Merteuil into the position where these experts in psychological analysis involuntarily analyse themselves and thus reveal their final inadequacy to the reader. In particular, it is in the unintentional self-portrait which madame de Merteuil offers of herself that her inferiority to the Présidente can be found.

At first sight, and on the scale of values which she herself espouses, madame de Merteuil seems to be the ideal of the sexually successful woman. She has escaped from the traditional passivity of her sex, and enjoys what is generally regarded as the masculine prerogative of freely choosing the objects of her pleasure. This is even reflected in her language, for while the colloquial words for the sexual act have always, as Anthony Quinton remarks, 'had the man as the grammatical subject and the woman as grammatical object',[12] madame de Merteuil concludes her self-portrait in letter 81 with the words: 'Quant à Prévan, je veux l'avoir et je l'aurai'. It is she who takes the initiative and who is the dominant partner in all her relationships. She is detached enough to make puns about her own and other people's immorality, and refers to the anecdote which supposedly inspires the *lettre de rupture* that she makes Valmont write to the Présidente as 'une histoire de perdue'(**141**). She is so free from conventional moral restraints that she can think of what is normally regarded as a sexual perversion with little more than an amused tolerance, and refers on three separate occasions to the interest which she feels in Cécile Volanges as a possible sexual partner (**20; 38; 39**). Yet while her lesbian tendencies can be seen from one point of view as an enterprising attempt to widen the range of her sexual pleasures, or as a conscious part of her war against the whole of the male sex, they can also be interpreted in a much less favourable light. When Valmont says 'je ne sais pourquoi, il n'y a plus que les choses bizarres qui me plaisent' (**110**), his comment suggests how promiscuity can lead to a jaded appetite and satiety to perversion. This is certainly the final impression left by madame de Merteuil, and her little joke about being a lost woman, while a witty and conscious description of her own character—as well as an entertaining anticipation of the Présidente's fate—is also true in a way that she does not suspect when she makes it. It is the letter that she makes Valmont write to the Présidente which ultimately brings about her own downfall as well as that of madame de Tourvel, and which, far from being a 'balle perdue' that misses its target, is a 'bloody instruction' that returns to plague its inventor. Had this letter not killed the love between Valmont and madame de Tourvel so effectively—'quand une femme frappe dans le cœur d'une autre, elle manque rarement de trouver l'endroit sensible, et la blessure est incurable' (145)—then Valmont would have been less determined to pay madame de Merteuil back for deceiving him with Danceny. Where her involuntary self-analysis is most visible, however, is in her use of the word *humeur*, and it is the contrast between her predilection for this term and madame de Tourvel's preference for *bonheur* which shows how consistent Laclos's values remain in the linguistic patterns of his novel as well as in the story it tells.

If success in sexual relationships is linked to the happiness which these offer, then madame de Merteuil is the most unsuccessful character in the whole of *Les Liaisons dangereuses*. Whereas it is the thought of Valmont's happiness which consoles madame de Tourvel even when she knows she is doing wrong (**128; 132**), the very word *bonheur* seems foreign to madame de Merteuil's vocabulary. She uses it very rarely, and on one occasion gives it a predominantly sexual but also a highly ironic twist when she tells Valmont that she is going to concern herself 'du bonheur de Prévan'(**74**). Her characteristic word is *humeur*, and she uses it at least a dozen times. It is bad temper which prevails in her reaction to Valmont's designs on the Présidente (**10**), which threatens to recur if Prévan does not attend a minor social function (**74**), which flares up when Valmont dares to give her advice (**81**), which she consciously uses as a weapon (**5; 113**), which she recognises that she feels on occasion (**121; 131**), but which she denies is ever powerful enough to affect her judgment (**134**). Yet although she promises herself, towards the end of the novel, that she will avoid bad temper in the future—'j'ai trop bien reconnu qu'elle pourrait devenir un piège'(**131**)—it is nothing but a violent and irresistible onset of *humeur* which leads her to make the mistake of telling Danceny about Valmont and Cécile.

The contrast between the positive values incarnated in the présidente de Tourvel and the essentially negative world view represented by madame de Merteuil becomes even clearer if we look at the one relationship in the novel where the Marquise seems to be thinking in the same terms as the Présidente. There is, on the surface, at least the possibility that the intense jealousy which madame de Merteuil feels for madame de Tourvel stems from the fact that she loves Valmont herself. Her regret for 'un bonheur qui ne peut revenir'(131)—again an example of her speaking better than she knows, since Valmont is by now in love with the Présidente—seems to support this view, and her loss of caution at the end might perhaps be attributed to a genuine despair at having lost the one man who could have made her happy. However, what is most significant about her statement to Valmont that 'dans le temps où nous nous aimions, car je crois que c'était de l'amour, j'étais heureuse'(131) is the context in which it is made. In this letter, madame de Merteuil is doing everything she can to draw Valmont away from the Présidente. She has tried to make him jealous by her description in an earlier letter (113) of her attempts to exhaust the sexual ardour of her lover Belleroche, and she is now using the reference to the happiness which she and Valmont once enjoyed together as an additional bait. However, once he has swallowed it and sacrificed madame de Tourvel (141; 142), there is no further question of the *amour* which the Marquise earlier suggested that she once had for him. On the very same day that she tells him 'je vous aime toujours beaucoup, et je me prépare à vous le prouver'(145), she makes an assignation with Danceny (146). The first part of her sentence thereby becomes a condescending reassurance that she is still quite fond of him—'je vous aime beaucoup' is, paradoxically, much weaker than the simple 'je vous aime'—while the second phrase is deliberately ironic: she will prove her love for him by becoming Danceny's mistress. Her behaviour at this point in the novel, when she might have a fair chance of taking Valmont back—on the rebound from the Présidente, as it were—if this were what she wanted, suggests that she has never really loved him, and is, in fact, quite incapable of experiencing happiness through love. She is capable only of the sterile jubilation procured by tricking other people and triumphing over them, and the idea of an equal relationship between two partners—the official and acceptable aim of all supporters of female emancipation—is quite foreign to her nature. She is evil both through what she does to other people and through what she is herself: negative, bad-tempered and self-defeating. When Swinburne described her as a 'Prometheus in skirts',[13] his phrase suggested that her revolt against male privilege was noble and justified. What she actually does in the novel, as well as a great deal of what she says, shows only how sour her revolt has turned and how she finally resembles, not the Romantic image of Lucifer, but George Bernard Shaw's more prosaic assessment of the devil as someone rather petty.[14]

*****

In the same way that the atmosphere of *Les Liaisons dangereuses* gradually changes as the action proceeds, so does the relative importance of the different characters. Once she becomes Valmont's mistress, madame de Tourvel ceases to be overshadowed by madame de Merteuil and triumphantly asserts her own values and personality. The two letters in which she describes to madame de Rosemonde the love which she now feels for Valmont (**128; 132**) are not only intensely lyrical and moving; they also show that she has the ability, so lacking in Valmont himself, to adopt new values when experience has proved to her that they are good. The happiness which predominates in these letters, both as a fact of experience and as an ethical value outweighing religious scruples, is linked with Laclos's revolutionary sympathies by the evident anticipation of Saint-Just's assertion, in March 1794, that 'Le bonheur est une idée neuve en Europe.' Valmont comes close to experiencing this happiness—'l'ivresse fut complète et réciproque; et, pour la première fois, la mienne survécut au plaisir'(**125**)—but lacks the ability to make it permanent either for himself or for the woman he loves. Madame de Merteuil brings him to heel in a moment by the suggestion that people might laugh if he gives up what is now only his pose as a *libertin* (**141**), and his reluctance to risk a few smiles is very different from the Présidente's total disregard for the much graver social consequences of her change of heart. She discovers the reality of love and happiness from a man who pretended to believe in neither, and it is this irony of events which reflects the sincerity of Laclos's Rousseauism. Yet she is killed by a woman equally incapable of loving and of being happy, and it is this triumph of evil which prevents the novel from having the happy ending that would normally be required of a proselytising work of art. For while the ambiguity of *Les Liaisons dangereuses* can be reduced by a detailed study of its language and style, the overall impression left by the book is much more that of tragedy than of optimistic social commitment. However, this may be less the result of any mixed feelings which Laclos might have had towards his characters than an illustration of a well-known artistic problem: that of giving a successful description of happiness in a work of imaginative literature.[15]

In this respect, there is some indication in Laclos's correspondence of how difficult it was to translate his personal vision of the good life into convincing artistic form. Immediately after mentioning his ambition to write a novel on the theme *il n'existe de bonheur que dans la famille,* he remarked to his wife that: 'les événements seront difficiles à arranger et la difficulté presque insurmontable sera d'intéresser sans rien de romanesque'.[16] He had, in *Les Liaisons dangereuses,* provided a kind of photographic negative of his ideal; and in order to do so, had used the conventional devices of duels, abandoned heroines, heartless seducers, multiple seductions and public humiliations. But precisely because the course of true love can, in a marriage like Laclos's, run remarkably smooth—after seventeen years of marriage, he wrote to his wife that: 'Il [l'amour] ne s'est même point partagé avec nos enfants, il s'est seulement répandu sur eux'[17]—there are cases when there is simply nothing to relate. It has been suggested, and there is nothing in the text of *Les Liaisons dangereuses* to go against the idea, that Valmont deliberately allowed Danceny to kill him.[18] After his discovery that the attempt to combine passionate love and heartless seduction can lead only to death and misery, Valmont has nothing left to live for and turns to Danceny in order both to escape from the world and to expiate his crimes. If this is so, then it could be that the brilliant Valmont dies in order that the dull Laclos can live. Laclos may not have known, when he began *Les Liaisons dangereuses,* exactly what his own value system was. He discovered it in the course of writing the book. Imaginatively, he lived through the ambitions of Valmont and madame de Merteuil, and imaginatively realised that what they stood for would not work. What did work, for him, was the placid dullness revealed by his letter, the blameless mediocrity of a man who now no longer wanted to dominate but only to be happy. 'Le bonheur', he wrote to his wife, 'est le but, la gloire n'est qu'un moyen.'[19] Valmont and madame de Merteuil mistook the means for the end. The Laclos who had learned from their mistakes did not.

Notes

(1)   Dard, *op. cit.*, pp. 386-9. Laclos's military career nevertheless showed that he lacked the one quality which Napoleon looked for in a general: luck. No sooner had he completed his training, and been commissioned as a second lieutenant, than the Treaty of Paris, signed on 10 February 1763, put an end to the Seven Years' War (and to the French empire in Canada and India), inaugurating a period of peace which ended only with the French participation in the war of American Independence in 1776, and more importantly, with the revolutionary wars of the 1790s.

On 19 September 1792 General Kellerman won the battle of Valmy, described by Goethe as the beginning of a new historical era. Our hero was not there, having been sent to help repulse the Prussian invasion of France and returning to Paris on 18 September. On 14 June 1800, just as his version of the exploding shell was ready to be tested in battle, Napoleon's victory over the Austrians at Marengo prevented Laclos from seeing it used in his lifetime.

His final posting to Taranto, as far as possible from the centre of the new empire which Napoleon was creating through his conquests, was scarcely a mark of Bonaparte's confidence in Laclos's ability to influence events. By that time, Laclos was sixty, suffered badly from piles (reference edition, p. 969), and had lost most of his teeth (*ibid.*, p. 989). He died as a result of dysentery and exhaustion, having worn himself out inspecting the fortifications at Taranto on a hot autumn day.

(2)   *Préface du rédacteur*, reference edition, p. 7.

(3)   See the extract from Tilly's *Mémoires*, Allem edition, pp. 707-710.

(4)   Allem edition, p. 704.

(5)   Versini, *op. cit.*, p. 310.

(6)   Versini, *op. cit* ., p. 251.

(7)   David Lodge, in 'The Art of Fiction: 5, The Epistolary Novel' (*The Independent on Sunday*, 23 June 1991), agrees that there is heightening of reader alertness and empathy, and could have no better support than that of one of the genre's most accomplished practitioners: 'The epistolary novel is a type of first-person narrative, but it has certain features not found in the more familiar autobiographical mode. Whereas the story of an autobiography is known to the narrator before he starts, letters chronicle an ongoing process; or as Richardson put it: "*Much more* lively and affecting [...] must be the style of those who write in the height of a *present* distress, the mind tortured by the pangs of uncertainty..."'

(8)   Reference edition, p. 5.

(9)   *Situations I: 'M. François Mauriac et la liberté* ' (Gallimard, 1947), pp. 56-7.

(10)   In the film, this is just *Christian Thoughts;* in the play, there is also reference to 'a novel written by some Englishman, *Clarissa.*'

(11)   Thus the fact that Cécile (see note 12 to Chapter One) does not even realise that she is pregnant, in spite of having missed two periods before her miscarriage, suggests that convent education is faulty because it leaves girls hopelessly ignorant about the physiology of sex. Here, madame de Merteuil makes the more probable criticism that young girls, shut up in a convent at a time when puberty makes them extremely aware of sex, become very knowledgeable about it, albeit in an unhealthy manner.

(12)   *The Observer,* 29 June 1969.

(13)   Quoted by Delmas, *op. cit.*, p. 463.

(14)   See *Man and Superman,* Act III.

(15)   As Gide's protagonist Michel discusses with himself at the end of Part One of *L'Immoraliste:* 'Que serait le récit du bonheur? Rien, que ce qui le prépare, puis ce qui le détruit, ne se raconte.'

(16)   Reference edition, p. 1064; letter of 8 April 1801.

(17)   *Idem,* p. 947; leter of 13 September 1800.

(18)   This is certainly suggested in the play, and is made very obvious in the Erroll Flynn-type duel.

(19)   Reference edition, p. 1002; letter of 25 November 1800.

Chapter Three

Critical Perspectives

Tragedy

Laclos's conscious reasons for placing his final condemnation of Valmont and madame de Merteuil fairly deep in the texture of his novel are not difficult to imagine. If the moral lesson of a work of art is too close to the surface, the reader sees it too quickly and dismisses it. If, on the other hand, he has to discover it himself through a close study of the text, he is more likely to congratulate himself upon his perspicacity than to condemn the author for subordinating literature to moral teaching. Laclos may well have been mistaken in relying upon the *salon* tradition of close reading and detailed analysis to lead his public to something like the interpretation set out in the preceding chapter, for critics have, in general, insisted either upon the licentious or upon the ambiguous nature of his work. Thus Laurent Versini, while arguing that Laclos's novel is 'la condamnation du libertinage élégant par un honnête homme et un disciple de Jean-Jacques Rousseau', admits that this interpretation cannot claim entirely to 'dissiper l'ambiguïté des *Liaisons*',[1] and even Baudelaire, the first to recognise the morality implicit in the work, never actually managed to work his brief notes into a sustained interpretation. It is true that he was planning to write his study of Laclos at a period in his life when he seems to have been incapable of finishing anything, and the rather scrappy state of his notes might therefore be explained by purely individual factors. Nevertheless, he may equally well have been held back by his awareness of how difficult it was to fit the novel into any systematic frame of moral reference, and it is significant that his famous description of *Les Liaisons dangereuses* as a 'livre de moraliste aussi haut que les plus éléves, aussi profond que les plus profónds' should be printed immediately opposite his quite contradictory statement that 'tous les livres sont immoraux'.[2] It is almost as if he could not choose between these two ideas and therefore could not really decide how to approach the book. This impression is strengthened by the contrast between his general remark that, in *Les Liaisons dangereuses*, 'La détestable humanité se fait un enfer préparatoire', and his more particular comment that madame de Tourvel is: 'Une femme naturelle. Une Ève touchante'.[2] For reasons that Baudelaire does not define, the Présidente escapes from its general atmosphere of perdition, and casts a zone of purity and light which quite contradicts the life-denying implications of 'la détestable humanité'. Her qualities are not, however, sufficient to enable her to triumph over the spirit of evil which is an equally real force in the novel. Her sincerity, simplicity and spontaneity are indeed admirable, but her virtue cannot withstand Valmont's experienced technique, and her spontaneity is killed stone dead as soon as madame de Merteuil decides to strike. 'Je vois bien dans tout cela les méchants punis', writes madame de Volanges to madame de Rosemonde, 'mais je n'y trouve nulle consolation pour leurs malheureuses victimes'(173), and her remark is strikingly similar to George Orwell's definition of 'the level of tragedy' in his essay *Lear, Tolstoy and the Fool:* 'Vice is punished, but virtue is not rewarded'.[3] It would, of course, have been technically very difficult for Laclos to have given his novel the 'happy ending' required of a genuinely moralising work. A reformed Valmont married to a divorced Présidente is almost as inconceivable as a Tristan living happily ever afterwards with Isolde, and the social obstacles would have been just as great in both cases. Yet if he had managed to overcome them, Laclos would have been going against that aspect of his vision which once made Giraudoux compare him to Racine, and which gives his novel more of the general spirit of tragedy than any other work in eighteenth-century French literature.[4]

The hubris which Valmont and madame de Merteuil show in trying to exercise total control over human emotions is punished by a nemesis which recalls the ethical content of Greek tragedy, and, like Ajax or Creon, they are struck down because they tried to go too far in asserting man's individual power. Hamlet's

> Tis dangerous when the baser nature comes
> Between the pass and fell incensed points
> Of mighty opposites (V. ii)

is also a remarkably apt comment on the fate of Cécile and Danceny, and the intensity of the Présidente's suffering is so great that she, like Ophelia, goes mad with grief. In Laclos's imaginative universe, as in that of Racine, there is no valid basis for human relationships based upon trust and affection, and the Présidente is ruthlessly punished for having relied for one moment upon human affection. Most tragic of all, perhaps, is the sense of waste. Valmont is of noble birth, intelligent, courageous and enterprising. However negative her attitude may finally appear, madame de Merteuil has a brilliant mind, a resourceful and independent character, and a philosophy of life which she has freely adopted and for which she is prepared to assume full responsibility. The présidente de Tourvel has beauty of mind and body, and an immense capacity for love. Yet all these qualities come to nothing, and there is no possible consolation for their loss. The frequent references that Valmont and madame de Merteuil make to the theatre (21; 70; 71; 76; 81) constitute a particular invitation to compare Laclos with Racine, and such a comparison seems especially justified by the similarity between *Les Liaisons dangereuses* and *Andromaque* on the level of both plot and atmosphere. Without madame de Tourvel, Valmont and madame de Merteuil might perhaps have reached some kind of understanding; and without madame de Merteuil, Valmont and the Présidente could well have attained happiness. Similarly, in Racine's play, it is the presence of Andromaque which destroys the love between Pyrrhus and Hermione, and the very existence of Pyrrhus which prevents Hermione from returning the love with Oreste feels for her. In Laclos, as in Racine, the characters are caught in a trap created by the combination between their passions and a particular situation, and even Danceny and Cécile Volanges, minor characters for whom no Racinian parallel exists, might have found happiness together had it not been for Valmont and madame de Merteuil. There is even, in the final impression left by the novel, something of the metaphysical despair which characterises Pascal's or Racine's vision of mankind.[5] Here, in a society which offers every possibility of happiness to its leisured class, the only use which people make of their freedom and privileges is to pursue an evil and self-defeating form of sexual activity. If the famous *douceur de vivre* of pre-revolutionary France can produce the vice and suffering described in *Les Liaisons dangereuses*, then Newman's phrase about a 'terrible, aboriginal catastrophe' lying at the source of all human experience seems to provide a more likely key to an understanding of mankind than the progressive and essentially optimistic philosophy which Laclos defended in his letters and other writings.

The essential difference between Laclos and Racine, however, is summarised in Jean Giraudoux's contrast between the physical aspect of sex in *Les Liaisons dangereuses* and its virtual absence from Racine's tragedies:

> C'est Racine aidé par Vauban... Alors Andromaque se rend, Phèdre surprend dans son lit Hippolyte, Roxane tue Bajazet mais repue, et Iphigénie, bien qu'elle n'ait rien à voir en tout cela, est

violée en passant. Tous les meurtres et tous les suicides de Racine ont lieu, mais après jouissance, et l'on ne décapite que des corps épuisés.[6]

In the history of French literature, Laclos is perhaps the person who gave the novel its final *lettres de noblesse* by showing how it could be used to express a tragic vision. In the history of human sexual behaviour, however, he is also the writer who used the promiscuity of the French aristocracy in the eighteenth century to make a number of social and psychological observations. The promiscuity which seems to have characterised the aristocracy of his time was, in many ways, different from the permissiveness of European and American society of our day. It was not primarily hedonistic, but was more closely linked to that cult of personal reputation which had come to replace the earlier and more heroic idea of honour. Émile Dard remarks, speaking of the characters in *Les Liaisons dangereuses*, 'séduire n'est rien pour eux, il faut perdre',[7] and Laclos provides a most interesting commentary on the decline and perversion of the chivalric ideal when he makes the marquise de Merteuil compare Valmont to one of the 'preux chevaliers qui venaient déposer aux pieds de leur dame les fruits brillants de leur victoire'(**20**). What Valmont is going to bring her is the Présidente's dishonour, and his opponent is not a man but a woman, a member of that gentler sex which true knights swore to protect.

This total reversal of the traditional concept of chivalry is itself enough to show how fully the French aristocracy had, in Laclos's view, forfeited its right to the privileges it still enjoyed, and *Les Liaisons dangereuses* is indeed a devastating attack on the nobility as a class. Yet the very movement of the novel from gaiety and elegance to despair and disease is also symbolic of the general decline which appears inevitable once sex is separated either from its natural function of continuing the race or from its more noble human accompaniment of love. The society described by Laclos is one where the natural fertility of the sexual act has become nothing more than a weapon: once Cécile is pregnant, madame de Merteuil's vengeance over Gercourt becomes both more certain and more enjoyable. Laclos never formally states the connection, but the whole implication of his novel is that a society where an excess of leisure is filled by sexual activity will very soon become a society where such activity can no longer remain an enjoyable end in itself. It will become infected with the aggression and lust for power which normally find their outlet in other social activities. Laclos's vision of humanity, whether tinged with Jansenism or not, and in sharp contrast to his official Rousseauism, is realistic in the rather cynical sense of the word: he does not expect people to behave well when the opportunities are there for them to behave badly. Unless their energy and intelligence can be channelled into some useful activity, they will waste their time and spoil other people's lives. Yet while he found a solution in his own life to the problems posed by the eighteenth-century equivalent of the affluent society, he did not succeed in expressing this solution in artistic terms and may, in fact, have not even been trying to do so.

There are indeed a number of reasons why his projected novel on the theme that 'il n'existe de bonheur que dans le famille' did not become more than a rather flattering idea in one of his letters to his wife. Once he had solved whatever private emotional problems he may have had by settling down into a happy, middle-class marriage, and once he had tried, albeit unsuccessfully, to satisfy his desire for action by the political and military roles he played under different regimes, Laclos did not really feel the need to write any more. Émile Dard perhaps gives too great an emphasis to the social message of *Les Liaisons dangereuses* when he claims that it was a 'pamphlet politique' which Laclos would never have written in novel form 'si la liberté de presse eût existé',[8] but it is unlikely that he had either the actual time or the emotional need to write novels once he had met Marie-Soulange Duperré and the Revolution had opened careers to talent. A more important reason for the absence of a positive counterpart to the essentially negative portrait of human behaviour offered by *Les Liaisons dangereuses* is, however, the apparent incompatibility between the tragic vision and the kind of society favoured by the middle class. For reasons which George Steiner has discussed in his *Death of Tragedy* (Faber, 1961), tragedy does not seem to flourish as an art form in civilisations that embody the middle-class values so favoured by one side of Choderlos de Laclos's personality: personal happiness, marital fidelity, devotion to one's children. Laclos's presentation of the Rousseauist ethic in *Les Liaisons dangereuses* is astringent to the point of being almost ironic. The quotation from *La Nouvelle Héloïse* which he places as epigraph to his novel—'J'ai vu les mœurs de mon temps et j'ai publié ces Lettres'—could be taken as a sardonic comment on the inaccurate portrait of society produced by Rousseau's idealism, while within the novel itself, Cécile Volanges's miscarriage is almost as providential as the accident which enables Julie d'Étanges to avoid the natural consequences of her misconduct. It is rather unlikely, however, that Laclos is deliberately satirising Rousseau's philosophy at any point in the novel. What is much more probable is that he is following out his own more realistic and tragic vision of how people actually behave. This vision produced, in *Les Liaisons dangereuses*, the last of the tragedies traditionally associated with aristocratic society; and, either consciously or unconsciously, Laclos realised that the values to which he held in his other writings, and which seem to have inspired his behaviour after 1784, were not compatible with the artistic tradition that he was following in *Les Liaisons dangereuses*. It was not that he was uncertain about these values, or that he was genuinely tempted to prefer madame de Merteuil to the Présidente. It was that he could not combine the philosophy of happiness which he held as a private citizen with the tragic vision that he had as a writer. 'Pas un seul ménage dans *Les Liaisons dangereuses*' write A. and Y. Delmas,[9] and the reasons for this, on reflection, are quite obvious: tragedy flies out through the window when domestic happiness comes in through the front door; and the presence in Laclos's novel of a happy marriage comparable to the idyll in the second part of *La Nouvelle Héloïse* would have completely spoiled the unity of tone which is so important in a classical tragedy.

Realism

The close relationship that exists in *Les Liaisons dangereuses* between the form in which the novel is written and the ideas which it expresses seems at first sight to preclude any discussion of Laclos's style and technique for their own sake. As I have tried to show in the second chapter of this book, Laclos subordinates everything to the depiction of character and analysis of motive, so that even the wit and elegance of Valmont and madame de Merteuil are used to encourage the reader to think of them in a certain way. Laclos is again in the tradition of classical or Racinian tragedy in his total lack of concern, as a novelist, for the external world. For all his Rousseauan sympathies, nature does not exist either for him or for his characters. If Valmont goes into the country to shoot, he is interested in trees and bushes only in so far as they hide—or fail to hide—the servant dispatched to follow him (**21**). Neither does the physical appearance of Laclos's characters seem to matter. We know that Cécile Volanges is blonde, but only because Gercourt has the ridiculous idea that blondes are better behaved than brunettes (**2**). But apart from Valmont's remark on how beautiful madame de Tourvel's teeth look on the rare occasions when she smiles (**6**), there are no physical details about anyone else, and no comments on society which are not directly related to the plot of the novel. When Cécile Volanges curtsies to her bootmaker under the impression that so well-dressed and well-spoken a man must be her fiancé—'"madame," a-t-il dit à ma mère en me saluant, "voilà une charmante demoiselle, et je sens mieux que jamais le prix de vos bontés"'(1)—it is only incidentally that Laclos manages to tell us something about the uniformity of social manners in the eighteenth century. To the reader brought up in the tradition of Dickens or Balzac, or accustomed to the wider vision of Fielding, Richardson or Rousseau, *Les Liaisons dangereuses* will inevitably seem to be offering only a very limited segment of human experience. There is almost the temptation to say that it is a mathematician's novel, as much in the total elimination of the apparent irrelevancies which make up the stuff of ordinary life as in the elegance and economy of its construction. Laclos has pared down the experience he is presenting to its absolute essentials, and it is perhaps no accident that the extreme intellectualism of his approach should be reflected in the comments to which his novel most frequently gives rise. Since they are so little distracted by other considerations, critics are inevitably led to discuss what the work means, and Laclos's principal characters are so obviously concerned with ideas that it is appropriate and legitimate to discuss them first and foremost in intellectual terms.

This apparent narrowing down of the range of human interest in *Les Liaisons dangereuses* stems partly from the exclusive nature of the concerns which occupy Laclos's characters. Valmont and madame de Merteuil are mono-maniacs in the sense that they are concerned with only one thing: the power which their sexual attractiveness gives them over other people. They are, in this respect, similar to the characters in the novels of the marquis de Sade, and it is now an established fashion in France to place the two writers on the same metaphysical and even literary plane. Both, it is argued, describe the terrible liberty of man freed from the restraints of traditional morality, and both present sex as the essential element in man's drive towards total, Godlike power. A less flattering but more justifiable comparison would stress the traces of the erotic tradition that can still be found in Laclos and which make Sade's novels so totally incredible from any realistic standpoint. Prévan, according to Valmont's account (79), performs the sexual act the nine times claimed by Victor Hugo for his wedding night before going off in readiness to fight a duel the next morning, and what is described as an 'étonnante orgie' then concludes his adventure with 'les trois inséparables' in a way that is strongly reminiscent of the psychological, if not of the physical complexities of Sade's *Les Cent Vingt Journées de Sodome,* a book which attempts to describe and catalogue all possible and existing forms of sexual perversion. Similarly, the devoted female servant who can also, at need, be blackmailed into seconding his mistress's perversions is a stock character in the modern erotic novel, and the guilty secret which gives the sadistic woman mastery over the man is not unknown either (81). Letter 96 also shows that Valmont has a strong element of emotional sadism in his nature. When he asks madame de Merteuil not to hurry him in his seduction of the Présidente since he wants times to savour the 'délicieuses jouissances' offered by the 'touchants combats entre l'amour et la vertu', he is almost on the same level as some of Sade's heroes. Nevertheless, the very last sentences in this section of his letter provide a perfect example of how Laclos's greater maturity and balance enable him to go far beyond the very limited vision of Sade. 'Ah! le temps ne viendra que trop tôt, où, dégradée par sa chute, elle ne sera plus pour moi qu'une femme ordinaire', is a totally inaccurate forecast of how Valmont will think of madame de Tourvel when she does become his mistress, and Laclos's ability to see that sex cannot be permanently dissociated from human emotions is a most salutary corrective to the views put forward in the *Cent Vingt Journées.* There, sexual perversion and the association of sexual pleasure with physical pain are not only described in considerable detail but recommended by a battery of philosophical arguments. Sade's characters are totally lacking in any feelings apart from sexual appetite and 'philosophical' curiosity, and never stop in their orgies to consider that any normal human emotions might be valid outside their totally closed universe. In *Les Liaisons dangereuses,* on the other hand, sex is important precisely because it involves the whole personality. Whereas Sade's heroes and heroines remain basically unaffected by the terrible physical experiences through which they pass, madame de Tourvel dies of grief. And even Cécile Volanges, the character nearest to the sexual automata found in Sade, is so deeply wounded by what has happened to her that she rejects all possibility of future sexual activity by going into a convent.

The fact remains, however, that it is only a second and more reflective reading of *Les Liaisons dangereuses* that distinguishes it unmistakably from the erotic tradition represented not only by the marquis de Sade but also by more amusing authors such as Crébillon *fils* or Andréa de Nerciat. Laurent Versini observes that a study of the manuscript of Laclos's novel reveals 'plus de corrections bienséantes que d'incorrections choquantes',[10] and Laclos is certainly a master of the decorous euphemism as well as of the genuinely witty double entendre. However, these are all literary devices belonging to the essentially minor genre of the *conte grivois* — the amusing but salacious short story — and there is a suggestiveness about Laclos's euphemisms which compares unfavourably with the genuine reticence and restraint of madame de La Fayette or Racine. The letter Valmont writes to madame de Tourvel while he is actually in bed with Émilie is a masterpiece of sustained ambiguity — 'jamais mon amour ne fut plus respectueux, jamais il ne dut moins vous offenser; il est tel, j'ose le dire, que la vertu la plus sévère ne devrait pas le craindre'(**48**) — but it is not verbal felicities of this kind which place Laclos in the first rank of European novelists. When André Gide, as noted above (p. 14), ranked *Les Liaisons dangereuses* second in his top ten of favourite French novels, it was with the proviso that France was not really a country of novelists, and in the case of Laclos's book it is not difficult to understand the reasons for his hesitation. More than any other literary genre, the novel is capable of presenting the whole range of human experience. In choosing to concentrate exclusively upon one group of people with one set of preoccupations, Laclos may have succeeded in writing the most Racinian novel in French literature, with everything that this implies in the way of emotional intensity and tragic atmosphere. He may also have written a book which admirably confirms Albert Camus's thesis that the dominant characteristic of the French novel is a certain monotony, a language in which 'tout se ramène à l'essentiel', and in which we find 'une certaine conception de l'homme que l'intelligence s'efforce de mettre en évidence par un petit nombre de situations'.[11] Nevertheless, he did not write a novel which gives the immediate impression of belonging to the greatest tradition. Like its moral implications, the basic realism and deeper literary worth of *Les Liaisons dangereuses* reveal themselves only after a certain amount of reflection.

Thus while it is true that Laclos offers nothing like the comprehensive social vision of a Balzac or a Proust, and little of the social or philosophical richness of Diderot's *Jacques le Fataliste* or *Le Neveu de Rameau*, it would be wrong to say that *Les Liaisons dangereuses* has no value at all as a picture of French society in the closing years of the *ancien régime*. Class rivalry is there in Azolan's comments on what he sees as the Présidente's obvious inferiority as a member of the *noblesse de robe*, and there is a brief but telling glimpse in letter 21 of the poverty and injustice of French rural society. Class, rank and wealth clearly play an important role in madame de Volanges's plans for Cécile, and it is assumed throughout that no one in the novel ever expects to have to work for a living. Danceny shows a gentlemanly reluctance to do the wrong thing when he tells Valmont that 'rien ne peut justifier un homme de mettre une fille dans le nécessité de l'épouser ou de vivre déshonorée, quand la fille est infiniment plus riche que l'homme'(**57**), but it is clear that a society where a young man expects to be able to support his wife by his own efforts is still very distant. Rousseau's insistence that Émile should be taught some form of trade to help him in the coming 'siècle des révolutions' is given an ironic twist when Valmont, regretting that he lacks the talent for theft which 'devrait entrer dans l'éducation d'un homme qui se mêle d'intrigues', comments that 'nos parents ne songent à rien'(**42**), and the whole atmosphere of the novel is one of a society where people have nothing to do. In one respect, of course, this is not historically accurate. The eighteenth century saw a determined attempt by the nobility to win back the commanding position in political affairs which Richelieu and Louis XIV had taken from them, and Valmont could certainly have made a career in the army or in politics if he had wanted to do so, just as madame de Merteuil could, had she felt so inclined, have been like Voltaire's madame du Châtelet and competed with men in the realm of science and literature. What gives *Les Liaisons dangereuses* its value as a portrait of how a leisured class behaves when its members lack political ambition or disinterested scientific curiosity is the immense importance attributed by Valmont and madame de Merteuil to what are, in fact, trivial objectives—'La stratégie pour gagner un prix très frivole'[12]—and this very frivolity is itself a reflection of the conditions which Laclos is describing. A social class deprived of its duties but maintained in its rights will behave in this way, its members competing in an activity that can affect only their private relationships with one another and not their generally privileged status in society. As madame de Merteuil tells him (**152**), Valmont runs no risk other than that of public ridicule from a small section of society if he fails in one of his enterprises, and it is clear that he will always remain, for the outside world, 'ce précieux appui d'une maison si illustre'(**163**). The less useful an activity is, the greater its importance for a class that has totally rejected utilitarian standards and replaced them by an absorption with personal reputation. The whole concept of court life at Versailles involved making the rank people held more significant than the work they actually did, and the behaviour of the characters in *Les Liaisons dangereuses* shows how this scale of values had corrupted even those members of the aristocracy who could afford to remain independent of the King. From this point of view, *Les Liaisons dangereuses* is more than what Tilly rather dramatically described as 'un de ces météores désastreux qui ont apparu sous un ciel enflammé, à la fin du XVIIIᵉ siècle'.[13] It is an example of critical realism, of the description of society from a politically committed point of view, whose implications extend far beyond the France of Louis XVI.

Inner coherence

The French writers and critics known in the 1960s as the *nouveaux romanciers* were of course right in their contention that not all novels could be judged by the criteria of realism established in the nineteenth century. *Les Liaisons dangereuses* would still be a good book even if it had no social relevance at all, and held together solely by the complexity of its formal organisation. What Flaubert, in a written remark to Louise Colet that Robbe-Grillet found most attractive, set up as an ideal of stylistic perfection—'un livre sur rien, un livre sans attache extérieure, qui se tiendrait de lui-même par la force interne de son style, comme la terre sans être soutenue se tient en l'air'[14]—seems peculiarly relevant to *Les Liaisons dangereuses*, and the novel studied solely as an experiment in the epistolary form. Realistic considerations would still not be wholly irrelevant here, since Laclos does make a serious attempt to overcome one of the main disadvantages of this form either by keeping most of the letters down to a reasonable length or by offering an explanation of how any particularly long letter happens to be written (**79; 86**). The interminable disquisitions of *La Nouvelle Héloïse* or *Clarissa Harlowe* are fortunately absent, and whatever similarities there may be between Valmont and Lovelace, the former does not have to limit his sleeping time to six hours a night in order to keep up with his correspondence. Yet although the relative shortness of the letters in *Les Liaisons dangereuses* does leave the characters time for action, the epistolary technique which Laclos exploits primarily for the purpose of psychological analysis also has the effect of creating an imaginative world which gives the illusion of being wholly autonomous. His characters exist only through the medium in which they express themselves, and a Valmont or a madame de Merteuil who did not write letters would have no existence whatsoever. Those who, like Émilie, Belleroche or Prévan, either write no letters or have none included in the volume, are reduced to the level of puppets as much by the silence thus imposed upon them as by the subordinate role which they play in the action.

Seen from this formalistic point of view, the action in *Les Liaisons dangereuses* is almost like a ballet, in which madame de Merteuil is always trying to replace the Présidente as Valmont's leading partner, and succeeds for a time, before ending the dance by suddenly refusing to keep to the same rhythm, in interposing herself between Cécile and Danceny. In this formal dance, the Présidente and Cécile both have something of the same role, both seduced by Valmont while trying to remain faithful to someone else, both sharing him without knowing it before finally losing him to madame de Merteuil, and even taking the same number of 'steps' in the sense that they both write twenty-four letters. There is also a potential similarity in the fact that Cécile is about to marry a man who sounds as dull as the président de Tourvel, and Laurent Versini gives his interpretation of the novel a very interesting turn by writing that the Présidente 'a épousé Solmes, en quelque sorte'.[15] The psychological novelty whereby it is madame de Merteuil, a member of the traditionally weaker sex, who manoeuvres Danceny as she wishes (**63**), who deigns at times to help Valmont out of his difficulties (**106**), and who is always ready to advise him (**113**), also provides some interesting variations on conventional themes, and the similarity of *Les Liaisons dangereuses* to a piece of music is heightened by the language which the characters use. This is uniform in the sense that they all belong to the same social world and write the same elegant, classical French of the eighteenth century. Even Azolan's letter is only slightly incorrect, and this one example of a less polished style only serves to underline the similarity among the other voices in the novel. Yet there are, within this pleasing uniformity, variations of tone, pitch and rhythm which serve not only to avoid any monotony, but also to further that analysis of character and motive which is, for all the formal perfection of his technique, Laclos's abiding preoccupation.

Psychology

Indeed, it is this concern for understanding why people behave as they do which informs the whole of *Les Liaisons dangereuses*, whether the novel is considered as an experiment in narrative technique, a tragedy, a cautionary tale, an attack on the aristocracy of the *ancien régime*, a defence and illustration of the art of seduction, a study of emotional sadism, an example of the Pascalian *misère de l'homme sans*

Dieu and of the implications of man's inability to 'demeurer en repos, dans une chambre',[16] a revolutionary novel, or a perfectly constructed satire inspired by impeccably middle-class values. Laclos wrote his novel at a time when the French language had begun to profit from the richer harmonics created by Rousseauist *sensibilité,* but had not yet lost that ability to distinguish between the finer shades of human emotions which was one of the major achievements of seventeenth-century literature. The présidente de Tourvel's plaintive elegies of absolute despair:

> Rien ne peut plus me convenir, que la nuit profonde où je vais ensevelir ma honte. J'y pleurerai mes fautes, si je puis pleurer encore! Car depuis hier, je n'ai pas versé une larme, Mon cœur flétri n'en fournit plus (**143**)

are in perfect contrast to madame de Merteuil's short, vigorous sentences and taste for clear distinctions:

> Je n'aime pas qu'on ajoute de mauvaises plaisanteries à de mauvais procédés; ce n'est pas plus ma manière que mon goût. Quand j'ai à me plaindre de quelqu'un, je ne le persifle pas; je fais mieux: je me venge (**159**)

and it is the difference between the two styles which embodies the gulf between the emotional universes that the two women inhabit. Whereas madame de Merteuil uses the Bible only in a rational or ironic spirit, explaining the story of Samson and Delilah (*Judges,* xvi, 19) in a way that would delight a modern psychologist (**81**), likening the Présidente to the poor man gathering up the crumbs which fall from the rich man's table (**113**; *Luke,* xvi, 21), comparing Cécile to Mary Magdalen (**63**; *Luke,* vii, 38), remarking how she goes and visits her friends in affliction (**63**; *James,* i, 27), and observing to Valmont that he is 'wise in his own conceit', 'riche en bonne opinion de vous-même' (**127**; *Proverbs,* xxvi, 5), madame de Tourvel's knowledge of the scriptures leads her into error by encouraging her to think of Valmont as a possible prodigal son (**124**; *Luke,* xv, 11-32); and it is her vision of the role which she might play in such a context that lays her open to his final attack.

Compared to the Présidente's inability, for most of the time, to speak in any terms other than those of religion and virtue, madame de Merteuil displays an extreme variety in the type of language that she uses. Her familiarity with the new psychology of her own day, the behaviourism of La Mettrie, comes out in her scornful reference to those women who are merely 'machines à plaisir'(**106**), just as her knowledge of the classics enables her to parody Terence's *Homo sum, nihil humanum a me alienum puto* when laying her trap for Prévan.

'Songez que *rien de ce qui l'intéresse ne m'est étranger*' she writes to Valmont (**74**), and the psychological implications of her direct or implied quotations become more obvious when her use of language is examined more closely. Whether she is describing the preparations which she makes for a rendezvous with Belleroche—'Je lis un chapitre du *Sopha*, une lettre d'*Héloïse* et deux contes de La Fontaine'(**10**)—or discussing the problem of overcoming Danceny's honesty—'il est si Céladon que, si nous ne l'aidons pas, il lui faudra tant de temps pour vaincre ses scruples, qu'il ne nous en restera plus pour effecteur notre projet'(**51**)—, she places herself so far above her literary sources that she seems to be mocking the very books which she is using. She shows this attitude even towards her beloved dramatists, making cavalier use of Voltaire's *Zaïre* to illuminate an incident with Prévan (**85**), and the first impression left by her use of literary, religious or philosophical sources is of a woman who, never being taken in by any form of intellectual activity, retains complete mastery over the language and ideas that she manipulates.

Valmont shows a parallel tendency to use a reference to prose fiction in a disparaging way when he speaks of Danceny as 'ce beau héros de roman'(**57**), and like madame de Merteuil, he is very fond of legal and financial metaphors. Reminding her that she has promised him 'une infidélité' to Belleroche, he admits that 'l'échéance n'est pas encore arrivée', but assures her that, if she is prepared to anticipate, he will give her credit for accumulated interest (**57**). This is similar to madame de Merteuil's later dismissal of the suit so assiduously pled by Belleroche—'hors de Cour, dépens compensés'(**134**)—but here again Laclos does not vary his style simply to avoid monotony. He also exploits the language used by his main characters to emphasise the difference between them, and it is particularly noticeable that madame de Merteuil does not dwell on her metaphors. In the same way that she prefers short, precise sentences to announce her plans—'Il faut vaincre ou périr. Quant à Prévan, je veux l'avoir, et je l'aurai; il veut le dire, et il ne le dira pas: en deux mots, voilà notre roman'(**81**)—she always pays her reader the compliment of assuming that her references will be immediately understood. Whereas Valmont, dwelling on his final triumph over the Présidente, indulges in a long military metaphor which takes him back from Turenne to Hannibal (**125**), madame de Merteuil has a lighter touch. Her description of how she and Prévan fell back on 'la tendre amitié', and used this 'drapeau banal' for their 'attaque réciproque'(**85**), gives a reminder of the permanence of the sex war which is all the more effective for being brief. She acknowledges that Valmont can be witty on occasion, but adds that this wit could just as well be replaced by 'du jargon'(81), and it is noticeable that he falls into a stereotyped mode of expression much more frequently than she does. He tends to be a shade pompous on occasion—'J'ai beau vous lire et relire', he writes to madame de Merteuil, 'je n'en suis pas plus avancé: car de prendre votre lettre dans le sens naturel qu'elle présente, il n'y a pas moyen'(76)—and his habit of inverting the normal order of the noun and the adjective qualifying it rapidly deprives this stylistic device of any real effect. Early in the novel, for example, it is by an 'adroite gaucherie' that he brings an 'aimable pudeur' to the Présidente's cheek, troubling her 'charmante candeur' and enabling 'le doux espoir' to replace 'la cruelle inquiétude' in his own breast (6), but although madame de Tourvel changes, as the action progresses, from being her husband's 'inconsolable moitié'(4) to being a 'sensible prude', a 'sensible dévote'(76) and an 'austère dévote'(138), the 'tendre prude'(138) is rarely described in any other terms. Cécile's mother becomes 'l'infernale Volanges' as soon as she excites Valmont's wrath, and even 'la femme à la lettre' is described as 'la secourable Émilie'(47). Although madame de Merteuil appears to catch a mild form of this disease in referring to Belleroche, in an interesting euphemism, as her 'infatigable chevalier'(63), and to Prévan as 'ce superbe vainqueur'(74) or 'le discret amoureux'(85), there is generally less predictability and more delicate irony in her inversions, and it is again fully in character that she should use short, vigorous phrases to remind Valmont of how superior she is to him in action and debate:

> Que vous êtes heureux de m'avoir pour amie [she writes]. Je suis pour vous une fée bienfaisante. Vous languissez loin de la beauté qui vous engage; je dis un mot, et vous vous retrouvez auprès d'elle. Vous voulez vous venger d'une femme qui vous nuit: je vous marque l'endroit où vous devez frapper, et la livre à votre discrétion. Enfin, pour écarter de la lice un concurrent redoutable, c'est encore moi que vous invoquez, et je vous exauce. (85)

In the duel between these two characters, madame de Merteuil always has a potential superiority through the fact that her enterprises succeed immediately, whereas Valmont's main ambition takes some time to realise. Yet it is the language which she uses that makes this superiority manifest, and even her occasional, very conscious lapses into the crudest terms—'ces femmes que vous avez eues, croyez-vous les avoir violées?'(10)—show an ability to reject linguistic conventions exactly when she chooses and when her argument makes it necessary.

Within the general framework of *Les Liaisons dangereuses,*

even a minor character such as madame de Rosemonde has her own personality, revealed in her case by her gentle, flowing style which is in complete contrast to madame de Merteuil's tersely-constructed phrases or Cécile's much more careless way of writing:

> Je vous attends ici sous peu de jours, mon aimable fille, comme vous me l'annoncez [she writes to the Présidente]. Venez retrouver le calme et le bonheur dans ces mêmes lieux où vous l'aviez perdu, venez surtout vous réjouir avec votre tendre mère, d'avoir si heureusement tenu la parole que vous lui aviez donnée, de ne rien faire qui ne fût digne d'elle et de vous! (126)

Her traditionalist acceptance of male supremacy is reflected in her opinion that 'l'homme jouit du bonheur qu'il ressent et la femme de celui qu'elle procure'(130), and this again forms an interesting contrast with madame de Merteuil's hedonistic and rationalistic approach. The different characters in *Les Liaisons dangereuses* provide a permanent counterpoint of contrasting opinions and tones of voice, with the result that Laclos's novel becomes, in this respect, an anticipation of Virginia Woolf's *The Waves* or William Faulkner's *As I Lay Dying*. Yet although Laclos is as accurate in his depiction of madame de Volanges as he is in that of the marquise de Merteuil, and takes as much care to ensure that Danceny remains as completely within his linguistic limitations as Valmont does within his, his concern for language is never wholly separated from his criticism of the people he has created. Madame de Merteuil adores the theatre and delights in legal images to the point of promising to weigh Valmont and Prévan in the same scales (**74**). Yet it is at the theatre that she receives her final humiliation, just as in the loss of her lawsuit is revealed her ultimate inability to control her own and other people's lives exactly as she wishes.

*****

Les Liaisons dangereuses is unique as a novel in the difference between the initial impact which it makes and the final impression which it leaves. What seems at first sight to be a witty endorsement of the amusements to be derived from sexual promiscuity turns into a highly moral criticism of this immorality, and what appears to be a cynical tale about frivolous people reveals itself as a serious treatment of some fundamental problems in human, sexual and social behaviour. That the *sinner* falls into the trap which he himself has dug is not a new idea (*Ecclesiastes*, x, 8), and the phrase in *Jeremiah* (xvii, 9) about the heart being deceitful above all things might have been written with Valmont and madame de Merteuil in mind. It is the wide variety of questions raised by Laclos's novel rather than the unimpeachable lessons which emerge from it that make the novel so inexhaustibly interesting. What, we ask when we think about what happens in *Les Liaisons dangereuses,* should be the right relationship between the sexes? If madame de Merteuil was wrong to rebel in the way that she herself chose, then what should an intelligent woman do in a society which places women in a constantly inferior position to men? To what extent can human beings control their life by reason? Were Valmont and madame de Merteuil entirely wrong in their attempt to control their emotions, when so many philosophers, from the Stoics to Descartes or Sartre, have given precisely this as the prime object of human thought? Can we ever claim to understand either other people or ourselves, and can the unpredictability of human life be virtually abolished by a combination between intellect and willpower? How should Valmont and madame de Merteuil have employed their leisure and talents, when the society in which they lived seemed to have so little need of either? These and many other questions rise inevitably from the novel, but not because they are ostentatiously debated by the characters. It is the events themselves which are rich in the kind of significance found in all the novels of the highest tradition: that which deals seriously with the ethical content of our social actions.

It is not difficult to imagine how Laclos would have replied to these questions, for his life is there to provide a comment on his book which it would be foolish to neglect on the grounds that literature should be judged in total isolation from the people who produce it. He believed that men and women should live together in mutual esteem, attempting to realise through their affection for each other and their devotion to their children something of that virtue which Rousseau saw as the one consolation for man's disastrous fall from the state of nature. Men should try to change society when it seems unsatisfactory, and should keep their intellect and aggressivity for their public life. Since it is men who have placed women in the subordinate position which they now occupy, it is they who should remedy the situation; and the first step towards doing this is to provide them with an education that is in no way inferior to the one available to men. Laclos's project for feminine education involves a course of study that is well up to Honours standard in any British university, and he is, in this respect, a more progressive thinker than the Rousseau who thought that 'toute l'éducation des femmes doit être relative aux hommes' and seems to have been little concerned with the independent status or intellectual development of Émile's future wife.[17] Men should treat their wives as equal human beings and not as pieces of property, and the fact that Laclos was not opposed to the idea of divorce suggests what attitude he might have adopted in real life towards a Valmont and a madame de Tourvel who managed to defy the society of their time.[18]

Yet as Gide and many others have said, worthy sentiments like this rarely make good literature, and the ambiguity so frequently presented in this book as an inescapable feature of *Les Liaisons dangereuses* has its advantages for the speculative critic as well as its drawbacks for the stern moralist. After reading Laclos's novel we are presented not with a set of answers but with a variety of questions, and it is in this respect that it is most truly a book of the Enlightenment. It foreshadows what is good as well as what is bad in the open society whose benefits we now enjoy, for it is only when people are free to choose virtue rather than vice that their behaviour can be called good or bad. Its perfect finish is aesthetic and not moral. Even when the reader has found what he thinks is the correct way to read it, *Les Liaisons dangereuses* still leaves him free to decide what bearing this reading may have on his own problems and situation. And the more he thinks about what these are, the more he is brought to realise that the interpretation which he places upon this novel will always be a personal one in every sense of the word.

The more extreme supporters of women's liberation will find in madame de Merteuil the model and precursor for the rebels of our own day, and see the fact that Laclos punishes her but restores Prévan to his place in society as yet another sign that no man can give a fair picture of woman's revolt against male supremacy. The more moderate critic will observe that the marquise is a very self-centred rebel, and note that her intended triumph over Gercourt involves the humiliation of Cécile, just as her duel with Valmont ignores any suffering inflicted on the Présidente. The historian of ideas will be tempted to argue that the failure of Valmont and the Présidente to organise the world in accordance with their own concept of rationality foreshadows the loss of faith in the rational ideal itself, and draw a parallel with *Le Mariage de Figaro*, where the plot depicts a comparable inability on the part of Figaro himself to arrange matters according to a preconceived plan. The admirer of the 'golden mean' can confirm his preferences by seeing how madame de Tourvel's faith in the values of the heart can, if unenlightened by an appeal to the critical intellect, be just as dangerous as

Valmont's reliance on reason alone. Those who hold a mimetic view of literature will see *Les Liaisons dangereuses* as a superb description of the way in which a privileged social class can destroy itself, and perhaps add to this reading the idea that human beings are so naturally perverse that they can use their freedom only to destroy one another's souls. Those, on the other hand, who regard the novel as a self-contained entity which can neither teach lessons nor reflect social reality, will find a curious vindication of their views in Laurent Versini's discovery that *Les Liaisons dangereuses*, far from being based on what actually happened, provided models for would-be but unimaginative imitators of Valmont.[19]

Notes

(1)   Versini, *op. cit.*, pp. 11 and 50. This recognition of the ambiguity of *Les Liaisons dangereuses* is less visible in the notes to the 1979 Pléiade edition. Here, Laurent Versini insists throughout on Laclos's debt to a whole tradition of moral thinking which looked for the solution to the social problems created by people like Valmont and the marquise de Merteuil in the action of society itself, and in what Versini calls 'l'honnêteté' (p. 1158).

(2)   'Notes sur *Les Liaisons dangereuses*', pp. 68, 69, 71, respectively.

(3)   *Collected Essays, Journalism and Letters* (Secker and Warburg, 1968), p. 298.

(4)   *Nouvelle Revue Française*, XXXIX, no. 131 (décembre 1932), 854-70. For another comparison between Laclos and Racine see Georges May's article *Racine et 'Les Liaisons dangereuses'*, *French Review*, XXIII (1949-1950), 452-61.

(5)   Laurent Versini disagrees completely with this type of approach, and describes Laclos as 'l'honnête homme le plus dépourvu d'angoisses métaphysiques et de préoccupations théologiques' (reference edition, p. 1141). This may well have been the case, but does not stop the text from making the reader wonder why human beings are so wicked. In this respect, as in others, *Les Liaisons dangereuses* is a very good example of a book which escapes from the conscious intentions of its author, and shows how limiting it can be to tie down any interpretation of it either to what we know of these intentions, or to the immediate atmosphere and preoccupations of the period in which he wrote.

(6)   Giraudoux, *loc. cit.*, p. 869. 'Roxane tue Bajazet mais repue' is difficult to interpret because grammatically tenuous, but the main thrust is clear: the reader should substitute protagonists created by 'ce petit Racine' (p. 863) for their tragic counterparts.

(7)   Dard, *op. cit.*, p. 34.

(8)   *Idem.*, p. 30.

(9)   Delmas, *op. cit.*, p. 360.

(10)   Versini, *op. cit.*, p. 56.

(11)   'L'Intelligence et l'Échafaud', in Albert Camus,*Œuvres complètes* (Club de l'Honnête Homme, 1983), IV, pp. 345, 346, respectively.

(12)   'Notes sur *Les Liaisons dangereuses*', p. 69.

(13)   Quoted in the Allem edition, p. 710.

(14)   In a letter of 16 January 1852; see the five-volume *Correspondance* (Conard, 1910), II, p. 86. Robbe-Grillet states, in *Pour un nouveau*

roman (NRF Gallimard, coll. 'Idées', 1963), p. 177: 'C'était déjà la vieille ambition de Flaubert: bâtir quelque chose à partir de rien, qui tienne debout tout seul sans avoir à s'appuyer sur quoi que ce soit d'extérieur à l'œuvre; c'est aujourd'hui l'ambition de tout le roman'

(15)   Versini, *op. cit.*, p. 600. See *Clarissa Harlowe*, letter VI. His remark would, however, be equally appropriate if the name were spelt 'Soames'.

(16)   Pascal, *Pensées*, 269 (Lafuma); 139 (Brunschvicg).

(17)   See *Émile*, Book V, Section lxxvii.

(18)   Dard, *op. cit.*, p. 43.

(19)   Versini, *op. cit.*, p. 48.

Chapter Four

The Play and the Film

As pointed out in the first note to Chapter One, the decision of Christopher Hampton to situate the action of his 1985 play in the middle of the 1780s is not justified by the text of Laclos's novel, where there is no basis for madame de Merteuil's remark in the very last speech of the play that she and her friends are 'more than halfway through the eighties already', or in the film for her hyperbolic teasing of Valmont over his delay in bedding the Présidente with the words: 'The century is drawing to its close' (screenplay, p. 39). *A fortiori*, then, there is no justification in the novel for the stage direction which ends the play in the shadow of the guillotine, accompanied, as Jim Hiley noted in *The Listener*, by 'sheets descending from the lighting grid to reveal the red, white and blue of the French Revolution'. Only one specific reference **(134)** is made to the social defects of pre-revolutionary France that may have led to this, and it is to the very general tendency of the law courts to favour a pretty woman over an unfashionable orphan.

The emphasis in both the play and the film on the portrait which *Les Liaisons dangereuses* gives of a society ripe for revolution is nevertheless fully justified by the tone of the novel as well as by its plot and characters. The opening (screenplay, pp. 1-3) of the 1988 Warner Brothers film, directed by Stephen Frears and based on the Hampton play, shows Valmont (John Malkovich) being prepared for the day by a veritable army of servants who fuss endlessly over his toilette. Not until the perruquier has powdered his wig are 'his intelligent and malicious features' revealed; then his sword is strapped on and he sallies confidently forth. Just as the elaborate curling of Jeremy Irons's moustache and hair, when he played the part of Swann in love in the 1984 film based on an episode of Proust's *A la recherche du temps perdu*, underlined the opportunities which his leisured social situation gave him to waste his time on unhappy love affairs, so the opening sequence of the film of *Les Liaisons dangereuses* emphasises the pointlessness and artificiality which characterise Valmont's whole existence. The same could be said of madame de Merteuil's, as the weapons of her female armoury are paraded: her shoulders are polished with crushed mother-of-pearl, scented cream is applied to her neck, and she is fitted with stomacher and bamboo panniers before being laced into her corset and sewn into her dress.

This film does not entirely avoid the risk of becoming a costume drama, but this is not altogether a bad thing. Laclos was, when his novel was published, regarded by the top aristocracy in France as an upstart who showed presumption as well as ignorance in the way he claimed to depict the life style of his betters. The same criticism could not be levelled at the film, which shows loving attention to detail in setting the action in the most elegant and sumptuous of châteaux (Maisons-Laffitte, on the outskirts of Paris). This, clearly, was how the aristocracy lived, and the contrast between the beauty of their surroundings and the ugliness of their moral behaviour could not have been made more telling.

The casting of Glenn Close as madame de Merteuil was aimed partly at ensuring that everyone who had seen her as a different type of *femme fatale* in *Fatal Attraction* (1987) came to see what havoc she could wreak in a different kind of society. It also stemmed from the need to give the part to an actress who looked intelligent, and could even be suspected of having ideas of her own. Her strong chin indicated ample willpower, and she retained enough physical attractiveness to make it understandable that Valmont might have other motives apart from vanity in wishing to keep her as his mistress even after he had seduced the delicious Michelle Pfeiffer. Glenn Close, however, was born in 1945, and the make-up artists made little effort to disguise the fact that she was a good deal older than Ms. Pfeiffer.

This very obvious difference in age introduces an element into the film which is not there in the novel. Although the reader knows from letter 5 that the présidente de Tourvel is twenty-two, there is no indication in the text that madame de Merteuil is any older. She may seem so because she is more articulate and much more experienced, but in the eighteenth century people married at a much earlier age than they do nowadays. It is the idea that Gercourt, at the ripe old age of thirty-six, is more than twice as old as she is that horrifies Cécile de Volanges, not the fact that she is going to be married at the age of fifteen and a half (**105**), which she would clearly see as perfectly acceptable if the future husband were Danceny. Madame de Merteuil could quite easily have been married, widowed, have acquired the experience which she talks about in letter 81, and still be no older than the Présidente. The novel itself gives no support for the idea, made inevitable by the casting of the film, that this is the story of an older woman determined not to lose her lover to a younger and more physically attractive rival.

The difference of physical type between Glenn Close and Michelle Pfeiffer nevertheless emphasised what is a central theme in the novel: the difference of personality and value systems between madame de Merteuil and the Présidente. The stage direction to Act I, scene 2 of Christopher Hampton's play shows madame de Merteuil to be very unfair in describing her as a 'frump'. It is merely stated that she is simply but elegantly dressed, and this exactly reflects the difference between the life styles incarnated by the two women. On the one hand, there is the elegance, bordering on decadence, of madame de Merteuil; and, on the other, the promise of a new kind of woman, and perhaps of a new kind of society, represented by the simplicity and emotional directness of madame de Tourvel.

Whatever reluctance Valmont's servant, Azolan, may feel in donning a 'magistrate's livery' in place of the more dashing clothes befitting the servant of a member of the court aristocracy, there is no suggestion in the text that madame de Tourvel is the social inferior of either Valmont or madame de Merteuil. Her husband is away presiding over an interminable lawsuit in the provinces, but they live in Paris, and she is received as a social equal by madame de Rosemonde, Valmont's aunt, as well as by madame de Volanges. What is underlined by her simplicity of dress, as well as by the spontaneity of her emotions, is the way she represents the kind of woman admired by Rousseau and by Laclos himself, one who has little time for the hollow pretence of a society which has reached a level of sophistication that leaves it no choice but to decline or reform. The reading of the novel as a clash of value systems comes out admirably both in the play and the film, and would have pleased Laclos very much. There is no call to dismiss an interpretation of a work of art for the sole reason that it reflects what the author set out to do.

The play and the film end differently, the latter more faithfully to the text, the former in a way likely to increase rather than diminish one's admiration for Christopher Hampton as a playwright, if not of Laclos as a writer. As the lights fade, and there appears 'on the back wall, fleeting but sharp, the unmistakable silhouette of the guillotine', madame de Merteuil insists that the game of cards go on. There is no mention of the loss of her lawsuit, of her humiliation at the Comédie Italienne, and even less of the attack of smallpox which not only makes her face as ugly as her soul, but also leaves her with only one eye. In the film, though, we see her being booed at the opera, and the last vision of her, as she wipes off the make-up to reveal the mottled appearance of her skin, gives the impression that something is seriously wrong.

It is true that when Glenn Close, playing Gertrude in Franco Zeffirelli's *Hamlet* (1991), agreed to appear as an even older woman—if the Prince of Denmark is thirty, she cannot be much under fifty—her skin tended to look rather similar, and this may mark the beginning of a new convention in the cinema, whereby a female character's inability to control her fate is reflected in a loss of complexion. But by inviting the cinemagoer with a knowledge of the text of *Les Liaisons dangereuses* to remember what happened to madame de Merteuil in the book, the film repeated the mistake which mars the end of the novel; unless, of course, it was merely underlining the idea that all pretence, like all the make-up, has been taken off, and that madame de Merteuil is now to be seen in her true colours. The play, much more sensibly, limits her punishment to the awareness that she has killed the only man she might have loved.

At the same time, the play reminds the audience what bunglers she and Valmont are. Madame de Merteuil uses the word in the first scene of Act II when describing the episode in which Valmont fails to take advantage of the Présidente's distress (Act I, scene 9); this prepares the final dénouement by showing him as beginning to feel pity as well as love for the woman whom she had earlier considered as merely another potential victim. However, the word 'bungle' comes to apply even more fully to her than to him. For she is, in everything she undertakes, a kind of female Attila the Hun, leaving ruin and destruction behind her. Emotionally, she cannot sustain any relationship, and the first act of Hampton's play brings into sharp and central focus something which Laclos mentions only in passing, in a footnote to letter 2: that she and Valmont first came together when they had both been abandoned by former lovers, she by Gercourt, he by l'intendante de ***.

It is consequently not an accident that both should be seeking to avenge themselves for an earlier humiliation. In their continual search for new conquests, each is illustrating the idea that all Don Juans, female as well as male, are victims of emotional if not of sexual impotence. It is only because they are unable to sustain a one-to-one relationship with another person that seducers are continually seeking new partners, hoping on each occasion that the person they have just met is going to be the one whom they will be able to love for ever. Valmont's and madame de Merteuil's constant quest for power is a symptom of their inability to find emotional satisfaction within any ordinary relationship, and the reason for this failure is particularly evident in the case of the marquise de Merteuil. Every man she meets is an opportunity for her to show how much cleverer she is, and every woman a potential victim. Gercourt may well have been tempted by Cécile Volanges's money, as well as by the hope of finding a faithful wife in a blonde heiress. But he may also have felt, after the affair which ended with his abandoning madame de Merteuil for the Intendante even before there had been any question of his making an advantageous marriage, that it would be quite pleasant to have a wife who was not so obviously his superior.

The omission from the play of Laclos's unnecessarily moralising ending has the advantage of emphasising the fact that it is madame de Merteuil's own actions which cause most damage to herself, as well as to other people. She is quite right to claim that it is she rather than Valmont who deals the death blow to madame de Tourvel, and to derive a sadistic satisfaction from her ability to kill. But she hurts herself almost as much as she does her rival, and as the audience leaves the theatre it cannot help reflecting that it is self-inflicted wounds which are the hardest to bear. The Marquise remains alive to ponder the fact that Gercourt, her original target, emerged relatively unscathed, that 'the best laid schemes of mice and men / Gang aft agley', and that a little more self-control on her part might have avoided the whole final catastrophe. All she needed to do was to accept the fact, when Valmont makes Danceny leave her for Cécile, that she had lost this round; but that vengeance, when it comes, is a dish best eaten cold.

The success of Christopher Hampton's play, and of the film which Stephen Frears based on it, is in marked contrast to the relative failure of earlier attempts to transfer Laclos's novel to a different medium. In March 1952, a theatrical adaptation by Paul Achard was produced at the Théâtre Montparnasse-Gaston Baty, after having been turned down by the Comédie Française, but found little success with either the critics or the public. In 1959, Roger Vadim collaborated with the Marxist critic and writer Roger Vailland in the production of a film with the title *Les Liaisons dangereuses*. It had Gérard Philipe as Valmont, his good looks already eaten away by the cancer that was to kill him later that year, Jeanne Moreau as a sinister madame de Merteuil, with a beautiful smile and an even more beautiful back, and Vadim's most recent blonde wife, the Swedish actress Annette Stroyberg, as the Présidente. There are some noisy jazz scenes, and a catchy little tune to accompany the brief idyll in which Valmont takes madame de Tourvel to the seaside, but the contemporary setting destroys the atmosphere of leisure so essential to the novel. Valmont even has a job, that of a high-ranking civil servant, and is toying with the idea of going to work for one of the big international advertising agencies in New York.

Neither Paul Achard nor Vadim took the rather odd but effective textual liberty of making Valmont tell Cécile that he had been one of her mother's lovers. The dramatic effect of this helped to make Act I, scene 8 of Hampton's play a minor triumph of suggestive sexuality, beginning as it does with the reassurance that since they are in Valmont's room, Cécile will be able to 'make as much noise' as she likes, and ending with the promise to bring Cécile's sexual education up to date 'with a few Latin terms'. Valmont's knowledge of how madame de Volanges had been warning the Présidente against him makes what may well have been a total fabrication on his part quite a plausible lie for him to invent, and the audience always finds the idea as funny as does Cécile. Adolescent girls are, traditionally, not unhappy at the idea of being successful sexual rivals to their mothers; and Valmont tells madame de Merteuil, in letter 110, that she *is* rather a giggler.

Christopher Hampton showed as much skill in adapting *Les Liaisons dangereuses* to the stage as he had done in 1982 when making George Steiner's novel *The Portage to San Cristobal of A.H.* into a successful play. In both cases it was a question of transferring the text of a novel into dialogue which had the concision required in the theatre, and of thus making the audience understand quite complex ideas. In *The Portage to San Cristobal of A.H.*, this was the notion, justified by all the perverted logic which one could imagine in the mind of a real Adolf Hitler, of defending the murder of six million Jews by the argument that this massacre did more than the action of any idealist politician to make possible the creation of the State of Israel. In that of *Les Liaisons dangereuses*, it was the paradox of how thoroughly unhappy human beings can make themselves when they have been given everything necessary to an ideal life; accompanied by the study of how sex, the life force, can produce death almost as easily as it can create life. Where Hampton also showed his immense competence as a theatrical craftsman was by accepting, from the very beginning, that Valmont and madame de Merteuil were going to have to meet face to face.

This is one of the major and inevitable differences between *Les Liaisons dangereuses* as a novel and any adaptation to the stage and screen. In the novel, Laclos makes Valmont and madame de Merteuil meet only once, when he surprises her with Danceny (**151**). For the rest of the time, because *Les Liaisons dangereuses* is above all else a novel in letter form, their only contact is through the written word. This emphasises the essentially intellectual nature of their relationship, which is one where what is said, and how it is said, is more important than what is done. For a novel in which sex plays so central a role, *Les Liaisons dangereuses* is remarkably free of sensuality. Valmont is clearly very good in bed, and there is perhaps a note of regret as well as disappointment in madame de Merteuil's remark to Cécile, in letter 105, that 'tous les hommes ne sont pas des Valmont'.

Cécile, she implies, is unlikely to be kept awake all night by future lovers, and there is the occasional hint that Belleroche, enthusiastic as he is, may not be quite up to Valmont's standard. But madame de Merteuil, like Valmont, is interested in sex primarily because of the power it gives her over other people. For her to be abandoned, as she had been by Gercourt before the novel even begins, is the supreme humiliation, equalled only by the possibility, which she recognises before he does, that Valmont is so attracted to madame de Tourvel that he may well end up by preferring her to the Marquise. It is because madame de Merteuil is so interested in knowledge and power that the writing and receiving of letters is so important to her. In this respect, as in others, she is an acute case of what D.H. Lawrence called 'sex in the head'.

Laclos was fascinated by the theatre, and makes Valmont and madame de Merteuil refer to themselves throughout the novel as being on the great stage of the world. When he was writing his novel, as Laurent Versini points out, Laclos quite often changed his letters to make them sound less like a series of dialogues that might be exchanged in the theatre. The novel consequently already had a dramatic framework for the adaptation to bring out, and the film occasionally goes a little too far in making explicit a number of parallels which are only suggested in the text. It is, for example, obvious enough that Cécile de Volanges is Valmont's pupil in everything without it being necessary for him to use her as a desk on which to write to Danceny as he had done with the convenient surface of Émilie for one of his letters to the Présidente. I found the play more satisfactory overall than the film, partly because of the greater importance of the spoken word in the theatre, partly because there is less temptation to dwell on clothes, furniture and buildings, but specifically because a play can more accurately target the audience which comes to see it.

The production costs for a film make it essential for the producer to attract as many cinemagoers as possible. This quest for a broad appeal involves a levelling down of particulars, and a consequent unfocused blandness. The film of *Les Liaisons dangereuses* was clearly intended to be seen in California as well as in Kansas, in Birmingham as well as Berlin, in Athens as well as in Adelaide. The play, in contrast, was aimed primarily at an English-speaking audience in England, and was all the more satisfying for that reason. Since the 1950s, and perhaps even before, English society has been living, as Christopher Hampton's play suggests that the society of the *ancien régime* was living, quite consciously on borrowed time. Every year, by some miracle, our own society survives, but every year the feeling grows that it cannot last. Something, somewhere, is going to put a stop to it.

The play and film productions

The Royal Shakespeare Company's production of *Les Liaisons dangereuses* has earned plaudits of greater spontaneity than the *Mail on Sunday*'s 'far more than a packet of French letters'. It opened in September 1985 at the Other Place, Stratford-upon-Avon, transferred to The Pit of the Barbican Centre in January 1986, in October of the same year (backed by Frank and Woji Gero) to the larger auditorium of the Ambassador's Theatre, and so to Broadway. Directed by Howard Davies and designed by Bob Crowley, its original cast included: Alan Rickman as Valmont; Sean Baker as Danceny; Lindsay Duncan as madame de Merteuil; Juliet Stevenson as madame de Tourvel; and Fiona Shaw as madame de Volanges.

Dangerous Liaisons, made by Warner Bros. (a Lorimar Film Entertainment picture of an NFH Limited Production), opened in America in December 1988.

Marquise de Merteuil	Glenn Close
Vicomte de Valmont	John Malkovich
Madame de Tourvel	Michelle Pfeiffer
Madame de Volanges	Swoosie Kurtz
Chevalier Danceny	Keanu Reeves
Madame de Rosemonde	Mildred Natwick
Cécile de Volanges	Uma Thurman
Azolan	Peter Capaldi
Émilie	Laura Benson
Julie	Valerie Gogan
Castrato	Paulo Abel do Nascimento
Opera Singer	Catherine Cauwet

Director	Stephen Frears
Screenplay	Christopher Hampton
Producers	Norma Heyman
	Hank Moonjean
Director of Photography	Philippe Rousselot
Music	George Fenton
Costume Designer	James Acheson

Running Time	115 minutes

Bibliographical Note

Laclos's complete works are available in a new Pléiade edition, with notes by Laurent Versini (1979), that supersedes the Maurice Allem edition. His *Lettres inédites*, edited and with a preface by Louis de Chauvigny, were published in 1904 by Mercure de France. The standard biography remains Émile Dard's *Le Général Choderlos de Laclos, auteur des 'Liaisons dangereuses', 1741-1803* (Perrin et Cie, 1905; reprinted 1936). The history of Laclos's reputation as a writer and moralist has been studied in detail by A. and Y. Delmas in their *A la recherche des 'Liaisons dangereuses'* (Mercure de France, 1964). This is an interesting study, but some of the attempts to establish an influence of Laclos on other writers should be treated with caution. Roger Vailland's *Laclos par lui-même*, in the 'Écrivains de Toujours' series (Seuil, 1959), is written from a stimulatingly Marxist viewpoint. A useful introduction to both Laclos and his novel can be found in Yves Belaval's *Choderlos de Laclos* (Seghers, 'Écrivains d'hier et d'aujourd'hui', no. 40, 1972), and this book reprints a number of his letters. Laurent Versini's monumental *Laclos et la Tradition. Essai sur les sources et la technique des 'Liaisons dangereuses'* (Klincksieck, 1968) places Laclos in the literary tradition of the seventeenth and eighteenth centuries.

There are, naturally, a large number of other studies of *Les Liaisons dangereuses*. J. L. Seylaz, *'Les Liaisons dangereuses' et la création romanesque chez Laclos* (Minard, 1958) is highly recommended, as also is Dorothy Thelander's *Laclos and the Epistolary Novel* (Geneva: Droz, 1963). Christine Belcikowski's *Poétique des 'Liaisons dangereuses'* is a useful account of Laclos in terms of some of the critical methods and presuppositions currently fashionable in France, as is Tzvetan Todorov's *Littérature et Signification* (Seuil, 1966). André Malraux's study of Laclos is now available in *Le Triangle noir* (Gallimard, 1970), as well as in the Folio edition of the novel. Madeleine Therrien's *'Les Liaisons dangereuses', une interprétation psychologique* sets out the problems very clearly and has a useful bibliography. There is also a very intelligent analysis of the novel in Vivienne Mylne's *The Eighteenth-Century French Novel: Techniques of Illusion* (Manchester: University Press, 1965).

David Coward's 'Laclos studies, 1968-1982', in *Studies on Voltaire and the Eighteenth Century*, no. 219 (Oxford, 1983), provides an excellent overview of the major books and articles published during the period when *Les Liaisons dangereuses* became something of a cult book. His judgments are more generous and open-minded than the dismissive comments Laurent Versini feels entitled to make about anybody's views that do not coincide exactly with his own, providing a reminder of how even literary critics give an unintentional self-portrait in everything they write.

Simon Davies's *Laclos: 'Les Liaisons dangereuses'* (Grant and Cutler, 'Critical Guides to French Texts', no. 68, 1987) is an excellent introduction, arguing that Laclos's characters are no more interested in religion than they are in politics, and giving a more sympathetic interpretation of madame de Volanges than provided by most critics. Patrick W. Byrne's carefully-crafted *'Les Liaisons dangereuses': A Study of Motive and Moral* (Glasgow: University French and German Publications, 1989. £8.50) is particularly detailed on the Valmont-Merteuil relationship.

Georges Poisson's *Choderlos de Laclos ou l'obstination* (Grasset, 1985) is a good antidote to Dard's earlier work, and argues that Laclos was slightly more successful as a career soldier in the army of the *ancien régime* than has commonly been thought. In 1982, a colloquium was held in France to celebrate the bicentenary of the publication of *Les Liaisons dangereuses*, and its proceedings, *Laclos et le libertinage 1782-1982*, published with a preface by René Pomeau (Presses Universitaires de France, 1983).